The Day My Life Changed

(An Accident Survivor)

BY

Linda Crosby featuring Roy Crosby

DORRANCE
PUBLISHING CO
EST. 1920
PITTSBURGH, PENNSYLVANIA 15238

Dorrance Publishing Co
585 Alpha Drive
Pittsburgh, PA 15238
Visit our website at www.dorrancebookstore.com

ISBN: 978-1-6853-7480-8
eISBN: 978-1-6853-7618-5

Dedication

This book is dedicated to
My husband, Roy Harrison Crosby, (Sweet Baby)
Thank you for always being by my side
From then and to now
God shone His face upon me the day I met you
Make thy face to shine upon thy servant: save me for thy mercies' sake.
(Psalms 31:16 KJV)

Thank You

To my family and friends and church family.

Your support over the years and now has made a difference. Your love, prayers, gifts, cards with words of encouragement, and your phone calls have comforted me. Sweet Baby and I could not have made it without the help of all of you.

These things I command you, that ye love one another.
(John 15:17 KJV)

Special Acknowledgments

All the glory belongs to God!

Stephanie Rose, my niece, who is like a daughter to me, and helps us whenever we need her. Stephfon Rose, my nephew, who is like a son to me, and was our chauffeur for a while. Stephfora Rose, my niece, who is like a daughter to me, and always lends a helping hand. Ashley Scott, my stepdaughter, who is like a biological child to me, and always set us straight. Rev. Dr. Eugene Burgess, my Pastor, and Mentor, who is like a brother, and is there for us day or night. Rosa (Rose) Burgess, my (deceased) friend, who was like a sister, and my sister in Christ, who spent countless hours on the phone with me. Sherryl Johnson-Hanna, my Registered Dietitian, friend, and sister in Christ, who thought it would be therapeutic for me to tell my story. Evelyn Johnson-Taylor Ph.D., my Writing Coach, friend, and sister in Christ, who made this book possible. Without her wisdom, expertise, and patience, this book would not have been written.

Contents

Prologue

Has an event ever occurred that changed your life through no fault of your own? One day, you are independent, and the next day, you depend on others. It is funny how you can go about your day, and out of nowhere, tragedy strikes. Your world is thrown out of balance, and nothing makes sense anymore. You ask yourself what now? Where do I go from here? Your way of living is altered in ways you never fathomed. Your mind has to adjust to make the changes you need to get through from day to day.

Even when you have doubts, trust others. Sometimes, things will not always go like you want them. You will need to trust the process and do the best you can. It will be difficult, but you need to move out of your own way. Kindness will play a key role. Just know it is a two-way street. Dark days will come, but the sun will shine, and you will smile again. There will be days when you will not have patience, but you have to be a trooper because it is for your own good. It is difficult for the people who are there to help because they are taking time away from themselves to make sure that you are okay. Also, most of them have their own family to care for as well. Let them help you win because they are the caregivers, and they know what to do for you. They have your best interest in mind and at all costs want you to get better. I know it will not be easy, but you have to do your part.

There will be days when you will want to give up, but you must keep fighting. If you are a person of faith, prayer will help. Do not let shame stop you from asking your friends and family to pray for you, too. There will be days when you will want to question God. Why me?

My mama brought me up not to question Him, so I never have and never will. The best way to get through a situation like this is to take everything in stride. In life, things do not always go according to plan, but we need to remain calm no matter what happens.

When circumstances arise out of our control, the situations do not have to overwhelm. Life is filled with highs and lows, so we ought to face them head-on and come up with a solution. There will be days when everything will seem to go wrong, and you just do not have an inkling about what to do. May I suggest you take a deep breath? Steady yourself, and try your best to remedy the situation. The answer may not come right away, but search and dig deep within to see what choices are workable to you. It may not always work, but do not let that prevent you from trying. You will be amazed what positive thinking can do.

It is heartbreaking when we become unable to live life as we planned. But we have to remember: If it is not God's plan for us, it will not work out no matter how hard we try.

Many people do not believe this. I do without a doubt in my mind.

I thank God for every day because each day is a gift from Him. Please do not waste time dwelling on what might have been. This can be very unhealthy and might lead to a destructive behavior. Trust God's will for you.

I had such a day on October 24, 2001, that changed my life forever.

1

The Accident

My Story

The sun was shining brightly, and the leaves were turning colors on the trees. What a beautiful day to have the windows down on my boyfriend's red two-seated sports car. I did not have a care in the world while driving through Lake City, a classic southern town on the east coast of South Carolina. It is known for its Tobacco Festival, an all-day family-friendly event. Downtown Main Street is lined with local people and tourists as far as the eye can see. Even the back streets have people milling around going to different arts and crafts show. The aroma of various foods is in the air. Music is blasting through the day into the night. And later, while I am lying in bed, then come the fireworks exploding in the distance.

I was born in April of 1959, and I enjoyed growing up there. Lake City's claim to fame is being the home of the late astronaut, Ronald E. McNair, who died during the launch of the Space Shuttle

Challenger in 1986. A monument has been erected for him in the downtown area.

My niece, Stephanie, had a doctor's appointment, and I agreed to pick her up. When I arrived, she told me she needed to send a fax. My boyfriend had a home office because he needed it for work, so we headed back to my house. After she was done, we started out to her appointment.

Traveling a familiar path, I came to the stop sign on Dansing Street and proceeded into the intersection. Out of nowhere, a car crashed into me on the driver's side. It hit me so hard, my head began to ache like never before. My car spun around like a top; I thought it would never stop—then it was on two wheels. Clamping down on the steering wheel, I tried to regain control. The pains in my hands and wrists were excruciating.

When the car came to rest, it was still on the same street, facing in the opposite direction. What just happened? Am I dead or alive? I was not sure. My mind was racing like a quarter horse, and my hands were trembling like an earthquake. Then came the fear, frustration, and anger. I had just wrecked my boyfriend Roy's car, his baby. He took pride in his car: He washed, waxed, and vacuumed it if a speck of dirt got on it or inside. He even sprayed the tires with Armor All Tire Shine. All I could hear in my head was Roy's police officer voice telling me to get the tag number. Piercing through the pains, the voice kept repeating, and I knew I had to get the information because if I did not, he was going to let me have it verbally later by telling me how crucial having it was for legal purposes. On that day, I did not know it, but this was the man I would spend the rest of my life with. Only God knew how much I would come to depend on him.

I tried to get out of the car, but my door would not open, I did not understand why, but I found out later.

Then my mind jumped to my niece. Is she okay? Because her son was only 21 months old, and he needed her. She is like a daughter to me; we have had an unbreakable bond ever since she was breathing. I can always depend on her for anything. She was also injured.

The firefighters were there in a hurry because the fire department is only a few blocks from Dansing Street. I knew the fire chief personally. We attended school together since junior high. Still in disbelief of what just happened, in my legs and feet, I felt only pain and numbness, I panicked and began hyperventilating.

Then the police officers came. They were there in a flash as well because the police department is also a few blocks from Dansing Street. The police chief was once Roy's supervisor, and I knew him, too. In a small town, it is easy to know many people on a personal level. After he completed the report, he asked me to sign it, but the feeling in my fingers were gone. What is happening? I wondered, so I asked my niece to sign it for me.

I asked the police chief to call my boyfriend, and please tell him what had happened. He did. After that, the paramedics came and transported me to the hospital.

I think the admitting nurse felt sorry for me. I was still hyperventilating. Unable to catch my breath, I became inconsolable to the point of hysteria. I was in so much pain and full of fear, she gave me a hug.

God always have people in place when you need them.

But little did I know it was the beginning of many hugs I would need. After being released from the hospital, I saw chiropractors for my neck, back, and pelvis. Then an occupational therapist for my hands. I went through physical therapy to walk again. But nothing helped.

After being referred to many specialists and taking numerous tests, I became cynical. Eventually, I was referred to the Medical University of SC, where they did a complete study, but my results were normal. I felt like a guinea pig. The pain had me in a living hell, and it turned my whole world topsy-turvy. I tried to get my boyfriend to leave because I did not want to become a burden to him, but thank God he did not listen. That is when I realized how truly faithful, kind-hearted, and caring he was.

My neurologist diagnosed me with fibromyalgia, a condition not many people were familiar with in those days. I was having widespread pain, tenderness, and fatigue when there was no answer for the discomforts. Today, I am happy to say advancements have been made concerning this chronic disorder. Twenty years ago, when my pain was excruciating, and I went to the emergency room; the doctor looked at me like I was crazy. He thought it was all in my head. This went on for four years until I was diagnosed by my family physician with neuropathic and joint pains. I was relieved to know that someone was finally listening to me.

The accident changed my life forever. I came to a defining conclusion: Life is fleeting and can be taken away in a moment. We need to make the most out of each day by living a life of integrity. My brush with death stirred things up in me about my mortality when it came to Heaven and Hell. My belief is, if life would have ended that day, I do not think I would have made it into God's Holy Kingdom. I was not a bad person, but there were just some things in my life that needed to be changed.

I have heard about people who decided to live differently and ungodly after an accident, but I chose to follow a godly path. My morning starts with a prayer, where I ask God for guidance for my day. This time in prayer gives me the spiritual energy I need for what lies ahead. Each day brings so much turmoil and evildoings, but I've resign myself to not let anyone or anything worry me that is out of my control. The Holy Spirit leads, guides, and strengthens me always.

After being in such a horrific accident, I was compelled to take full stock of my life. Prior to that, I was nonchalant about a lot of things. The accident taught me to appreciate what I have instead of what I wanted. Prior to that day, if I liked a particular style of clothing or shoes, I had to have them in every color. I was never satisfied until my desire was filled. After the accident, my heart was filled with more compassion for my fellow man. I now take the time to let my loved ones know how much they mean to me.

Before the accident, I was not too big on giving, even to the church; now I am a cheerful and willing giver to our church. It was like I had an epiphany to be a better person. When Roy, his nickname is Sweet Baby, and I can be of help to someone, we are. We give to others without looking for personal gain. My daily prayer is to do God's will and His way as much as I possibly can.

The accident showed me the true meaning, and gave me clear understanding of, living life to the fullest. I am more aware and appreciate what little time we have here on Earth. It was the scariest day of my life, and it took so much from me. Each day, I am still trying to catch my bearings, but I am grateful to be alive. My life will never be the same; it took me some time to come to grips with that realization. It was a difficult road to travel, and in some regards, it is still hard because in a split-second my life changed forever.

Everything had to be rearranged to accommodate my disabilities. My home had to have a makeover inside and outside, and I did not like it. The changes were a reminder to me of how my life has been transformed. It was hard, but over the years, I have come to accept those changes as well.

Honestly, I wish I could go back and change the events of that day. It would be great to have my independence again. I know life happens to all of us, and we have to learn to be content. But still, I wished I had never left my house that day. If I had stayed inside of my four walls, my world would not be turned into what it is now. There I go wishful thinking again; it can only lead to frustration for me. I had always been the kind of person who did not want to know what was in store for me. I like surprises. Boy, did I ever get a big one that day. It was not the kind I was expecting. It was more of a nightmare, and sometimes, I feel like I have not awakened yet.

We do not have a way to look into the future; we are living one day at a time.

My faith keeps me strong, but I am struggling on a daily basis. I was versed about the Father, Son, and Holy Spirit, the Holy Trinity, a long time ago, and He has been my Sustainer. God has carried me through dangers seen and unseen, and so much more. I am still in His bosom, which makes me think of the poem, "Footprints in the Sand." Being a Christian keeps me riveted on Him. Growing up, I should have read the Book of Proverbs in the Holy Bible because it is a road map for living. Maybe if I had read it, I probably would not have gone astray from my religious beliefs. I prefer the King James Version.

It is easy to see things in the rear-view mirror. If only life worked that way. Unfortunately, we cannot go back in time; we have to keep moving and do the best we can each day.

The past helped shape my present, so I have learned how to never forget. I am waiting patiently for the future. It was not easy for me to get there, but I have through Him. It has and continues to be a day-to-day journey. Some days are worse than others, but God is carrying me every step of the way.

When you are recovering from a life changing event, farsightedness is needed because looking ahead gives you a direction in which to go. You need to come up with ways to make life easier for you, and your caregiver(s). There are many physical and mental avenues you have to take to reach your destination. But let it be ingrained in you to try and make a full recovery, even if your physical and mental health are not restored as before. Do not be deterred by anyone or anything. When things in life seemed insurmountable, you must not quit. Though it is easy to just want to lie down and surrender, you cannot because life never stops. Gear up and give it all you have. Sometimes, it works, and then again, it falls flat. But be consistent in your goal of wanting to bounce back and do all you can to achieve your desired result. When your journey is long and tedious, keep going, because at the end of it, you will know you did everything required of you. There are times when it pays off, so do not listen to the nagging little voice in your head telling you to stop. If you miss the mark, at least you tried. The gist of the matter is to carry on.

The accident brought my being active to a halt, and I know I will never be that way again. When I was in the military, there were physical activities—running, jumping, marching, etc. I was in good shape, because we had to do physical training (PT) every morning in formation after roll call. After leaving the service, I stayed active for a long time.

When I went to dances at different nightclubs during my high school years, I did every popular dance at that time. There was this particular one called the bump. I was so good at doing it, I would go all the way down to the floor and back up again. I did many dance moves, too numerous to recount. Also, when I was in the military, I went to dances because going to them was a pastime of mine.

Gathering the pieces of what I am left with after the accident and conforming to my new lifestyle is ongoing.

2

My Prayer for Accident Victims

Dear Heavenly Father,

I pray for the reader of this book. It is my sincere hope the accident victims know You are with them and they are never alone. I pray You will strengthen them mentally and physically each day. Help them realize You will never leave them nor forsake them, even though these are trying times. Please give them good people who can support them in whatever capacity they need. Help them be loving and kind to the people who are there to make their lives easier. And help the people be kind and try to understand them by reassuring and regarding them firstly, because they are going through a new season of changes.

Please let them be thick-skinned, so if any disparaging remarks are made, they do not become heartsick from them. Help them understand things are not always as they are perceived. Sometimes they may hear and think things mean something they do not. Please give them the forethought to ascertain the truth before they form an opinion. Let them know it is very easy to misconstrue good intentions when they are depending on others for their wellbeing because they are in a vulnerable state of being and mind, so be careful not to make something out of nothing.

Help them know they have to do their part. Help them realize their lives might be forever changed. And help them understand sometimes changes are for the better even though it may not seem that way now. Let them know they maybe plagued with uncertainties, but to keep soldiering on.

Please do not let the changes weaken them for the rest of their lives. Help them find ways to conform to their new manner of living. Let them know it will take some getting used to doing things differently, but they can prevail. Help them realize at first it is like a culture shock, but eventually, they will come to accept their new life. Help it be clear to them progression will not be done without the right frame of mind. Always help them feel Your presence, so they will know Your love is never absent. And help them keep You in their hearts, so they will not fear.

In Jesus' name,

Amen.

3

Adjustments to Daily Living

As a result of the accident that nearly took my life, I became permanently and totally disabled, and completely dependent upon my boyfriend, Sweet Baby, for everything. Life as we knew it was over. The accident interrupted our day-to-day running of the home. Before, we had different functions within the house. He was responsible for the grocery shopping, cooking, dishwashing, and ironing. I did the laundry, making the beds, vacuuming, etc. I was meticulous about the cleaning of our home.

When I was able to do my housework, I took pride in folding the clothes; I was in the U.S. Army, so I was always organized and was taught how to not take up a lot of space, so I even rolled our socks. When I made the beds, I did hospital corners. I did everything like I had done on active duty. My chores at our home also consisted of dusting, and mopping.

Our home was immaculate. After I left the military many years later, I worked in the hospitality industry as a supervisor, so I knew about thorough cleaning. I rarely deviated from my usual routine. I worked Monday through Friday and did all my chores on Saturday. I got up early in the morning to start my day because we would always go out of town, even if only for a few hours, and I did not want anything to prevent us from going.

Then it was all gone in a flash.

At first, when I could no longer do my tasks, I was distraught because, for them to be done right, I had to do them. That was my mindset at the time. When I could not get things done to my liking, it was devastating to me because I wanted them done in a specific way.

Now Sweet Baby had to do it all, and it saddened me to the core because I was unable to help him. He does a good job and I am thankful, but I liked the way things used to be done. I did not like a lot of changes. Once, I lost a job promotion because of my unwillingness to change. I guess I was just set in some of my ways, but had to do better. I asked myself, How am I going to manage? Is he still going to want me? Everything was thrust upon him. I thought I was a burden; we were not even married yet. He assured me I was not, and he still wanted me to be his wife.

Before Sweet Baby and I were married, I had to have a partial hysterectomy because of internal bleeding. And before the surgery was performed, a tube had to be run up my nose down into my stomach to drain the contents of my belly. I saw everything going into a machine next to my bedside. Later, I was told that an appendectomy also had to be done because my appendix was about to rupture. I did not know how sick I was. Four years later, I had a complete hysterectomy, so I knew we would not be able to have children, but I never had let that bothered me until after the accident. Now with my disabilities, my body was a foreign object, and I was fighting a battle in my head. Will it be too much for him? I questioned my relationship because I was not a part of it anymore physically and mentally. What good was I to him? Why was he sticking around? I was riddled with anxiety. Am I going to face life alone like this? Will it be fair to marry him?

Inside, I was dying and felt broken beyond repair. I read books of certain Christian authors, biblical insights for women, and other spiritual materials, searching for self-worth. Also, I sought out books and pamphlets about less stress and more peace. I was looking for ways to relax my mind, body, and soul. But without a doubt, my guiding light is God's Word because I find any problems or situations I have and have had to encounter, the solutions are found there and in my prayers.

We need to trust, and believe, and never doubt Him, and when we pray, we leave our fears and burdens in His hands.

It is easy to become complacent with life and think everything is going to stay the same. I know now that is not the truth; when you least expect it and have begun to take all for granted, it can be interrupted.

After the accident, every day it seemed like a new problem emerged; Sweet Baby and I had no time to be fainthearted, and we met them head-on. It was not easy, but we knew what had to be done. The difficulties we faced were unimaginable until we established a system that worked for both of us.

The accident ransacked me. It sneaked into my life like a thief and stole my normalcy. It left me tattered. I asked, Serenity, where are you?

After seeing so many doctors, exhaustion became my constant companion. It is a never-ending cycle because I am still seeing some of them today. I get so tired of doctors' appointments and taking medications, but that is my life because I am in this broken body. And because I am in this fragile state of mind, some days, it is still hard for me to mentally grasp my situation. Why can I not live in a healthy body? This is a fantasy of mine. Sometimes I have dreams where I am normal; then, to my disappointment, nothing has changed. Keep forging ahead, my inner voice tells me, because that is the only way to get through these very trying times. My belief is, when I make it into Heaven, I will be whole again. The doctors can only prescribe medications, and they have done all they can do.

My orthopedic surgeon diagnosed me with bilateral carpal tunnel syndrome. On May 23, 2002, I had surgery on my right hand, and three months later, surgery on my left one. Even though I had surgeries on them, they are still very painful because of permanent nerve damage. I have to wear braces on both hands.

When I went to the hospital for my right-hand carpal tunnel surgery, I cried like a baby. When the nurse tried to insert the needle into my hand, my veins would not cooperate. She called them running veins because it was hard to find a good vein to insert the needle. I got stuck so many times I lost count. After the ordeal, I thought my hand would get better, but it did not. To date, I am unable to use the hand I was born to write with and to do other things. Also, my left-hand surgery was painful, and to top it off, I caught shingles after I was released from the hospital. When I had shingles, my hand was swollen two times the normal size. It was very painful, and the palm had red itchy blisters that oozed, and when they oozed, that caused more blisters to form. After awhile, the swelling went down, and the blisters crusted over. Also, I had a fever and chills. When my shingles got under control, I discovered my left hand was now the dominant one. I could not use my hands to brush my teeth with my regular toothbrush, so my husband bought an electric one. I use my left hand for oral care because the nerves are so badly damaged in my right. When you have been right-handed for most of your life, it takes some getting used to doing things differently.

Over the years, it has become natural because now I do everything with my left hand as if I used it from the start.

The muscle weakness and pain in my hands make it hard to grip things. I cannot write my own name, button my blouse, and zip my pants. I have to use plastic utensils to eat with and plastic cups to drink because they are lightweight. After the surgeries, I thought things would be better, but I was wrong. Since living like this for so long, I do not let it bother me anymore. Sweet Baby is very patient and understanding. I pray for God to strengthen him always.

Having bilateral carpal tunnel syndrome limits me from doing normal things. Sometimes the pain, tingling, and numbness are unbearable, which makes it difficult to eat and drink. It is hard for me to open my hands. My fingers get stiff, and I cannot stretch them out. Sometimes, they are so swollen, they look like links of sausages. Most of the time, it feels like an electric current is running through them. The pain and numbness go up into my shoulders. My braces keep me from bending my wrists because they are painful, too. I commanded my hands to work, but they would not listen, so I shouted, "What is wrong with you? Why can you not cooperate with me? There are things I need and want to do; you are holding me back." Then I said to myself, At least you have hands, there are people who do not have them. Thank You, Lord. I am grateful for what I have.

Later, I found out it is healthy for your mental state to be open for changes because nothing remains the same. Things can change without warning; always be ready for the unexpected.

I am able to write this book by using a speech to write program. ... Modern technology, what can I say?

My husband bathed, dressed, and fed me, and still has to assist because of my physical limitations and disabilities. Through trials and errors, we found a routine that was beneficial for both of us, and we stuck to it painstakingly. There were days when I had doubts and did not trust the process, but Sweet Baby would not entertain my craziness. After a while, I gave in and settled down. My dislike of a situation shows on my face by wrinkling my brows. This is a dead giveaway to him and has led to confusion many times because of mistrust on my part. But we always come back together as one. Now our routine is like second nature and runs smoothly. Every day is still a struggle for me, but at least we know how to get things done, so life is tolerable.

When you are permanently and totally disabled, one thing after another with your health happens. Because you are unable to take care of yourself like before, it becomes a spiraling downward. It is a very sad time when this occurs because things that were so commonplace have now become major tasks. Bathing cannot be done alone, and neither can you dress yourself. These two main private things—and so much more—are in the past.

Because of arthritis in my hips and sciatic nerve pain, I was confined to a wheelchair on February 25, 2005. It was hard to believed what the orthopedic surgeon said when he told us how it was going to be. It is funny how you take walking for granted until you cannot walk anymore. My feelings were mixed about my wheelchair at first because it was a blessing and a curse. A blessing because I could not move around on my own anymore, and a curse because it reminded me of what was to come. I could not stop the tears from flowing when I thought about how my life turned out. Reality sank in: This is my new normal, how will I manage? My husband has to push me in this thing everywhere we go.

I could not go to the bathroom; therefore, I had a bedside potty, and it was so humiliating.

Every time I looked at it, I cried. What is going to happen to me? I thought. This is not how my life is supposed to be. How much lower can I go? Lord, please help me to at least get back to being able to go into the bathroom.

My husband bought a power chair on June 20, 2008, so I could move throughout our home. It was a test because the chair had to be operated using my left hand. I was right-handed before the accident, and the nerves are badly damaged in both hands, but more in the right. Over the years, I learned how to use the power chair through trials and errors. Now with the assistance of my husband, I am able to use my power chair to get to the bathroom. Do not tell me God is not a prayer answerer.

Both chairs have been a godsend to my husband and me because life would be unbearable without them. There was a point of unrest in our home, but thank God it came to an end. My husband still has to use my manual wheelchair to move me around because of my handicaps; for instance, when he takes me to my doctors' appointments. He is now permanently disabled, too; he has cancer among other illnesses, but by God's grace, we are enduring.

I have muscle weakness in my arms and legs (joint). Sharp pains and inflammation in my joints cause limited range of motion, which in turn causes edema to set in. Edema is just another name for swelling. My muscles are stiff and weak due to me being inactive because of chronic pain and fatigue. It is hard to get out of bed or get up from a sitting position even though my husband assists me. When getting up from sitting, my legs, ankles, and feet are swollen, and feel like 10-pound weights are on them. Having debilitating joint pain is crippling.

When you are in pain every day, it consumes you. It takes over your life.

It robs my mind, body, and soul.

I have cervical neck pain and sciatic nerve pain in my back, every day. The pains are so bad, sometimes, I cannot lift my head. I cannot turn my neck from left to right and up and down without experiencing excruciating pain. I am unable to do any prolonged sitting or standing because I ache from my back down to my tailbone.

I find the joint pains I suffer from is worst on cold, damp, and rainy days. My body lets me know about such weather conditions. This is a fact not all in my head, but in every fiber of my being. During these times, the pains get worse. My muscles get stiffer, and I cannot move, even with the assistance of my husband. So, I tell Sweet Baby, "My body has locked up on me. That means no getting out of bed at all." I am grateful for my television because it keeps me company at all times, but especially on those days. My husband knows to pay the electric and cable bills if nothing else because I need my entertainment.

I have reduced bone mass in my hips (osteopenia), so I have to take a pill once a month, and it causes excruciating pain throughout my body. On any day, I cannot get out of bed by myself without the help of my husband. But during this time, I am more immobilized than usual, so I have to stay in bed. I hate taking the pill, but it cannot be avoided because my doctor said I need it to prevent osteoporosis. It is dreadful for me when that time of month rolls in. I do not believe I will ever get used to it, but if I had to take it daily, I would be in worse shape. Thank God it is just once a month.

Also, my pelvis got damaged. It pains me so badly sometimes. During that time, when Sweet Baby gets me in and out of the bed, I scream out loud because the pain is so excruciating. Words cannot explain the agony.

It would be wrong for me not to mention my eyes.

I have a cataract on my left and right eye, a floater on my left eye, and dry, watery, and itchy eyes nowadays. So far, I do not need surgery because each year my vision remains the same. Right now, I am prescribed a bedtime gel and lubricant drops. Since I was 10 years old, I have been wearing eyeglasses, and back then, I was called four eyes. During junior high and high school, I did not wear my glasses for vanity reasons. I did not have any other choice but to wear them while I was in the military. When I got discharged from the service, I took them off and did not put them on again until many years later.

Now with the writing of my book, I cannot do without my glasses because I am nearsighted, and everything would be blurry. It is not easy looking through these eyes. I pray to God, please let me see this book to completion.

Please listen closely to your healthcare provider(s) concerning anything that pertains to your health and provide as much information as you can because in the long run it might save you money, time, and effort.

> But the God of all grace, who hath called us unto his eternal glory by Christ Jesus, after that ye have suffered a while, make you perfect, stablish, strengthen, settle you. To him be glory and dominion for ever and ever. Amen. (1Peter 5:10-11 KJV)

Suffering is a part of Sweet Baby's and my life, but I know trouble does not last always. That is why this Scripture pertains to us.

4

Neuropathy

Most people think when you are disabled from a car accident, you must have had broken bones and had to undergo multiple surgeries to mend them. My disability comes from chronic nerve pain and all the other conditions associated with it, which makes the disability just as tragic. It is a vicious circle.

Neuropathy is pain of the peripheral nervous system that is unrelenting, debilitating, disabling, and makes my life a struggle every day. Prescription medications alleviate the pain, but it never goes away. Neither does the burning, numbness, and tingling sensations. It is easy for me to be unfocused because I am in constant chronic nerve pain, along with the other sensations, and I am only thinking about when my next dose of prescription drugs is. I thank God Sweet Baby must administer my medicines now. Due to me being scatterbrained, I might accidentally overdose. He makes sure I take them as prescribed. When you get to the chapter on depression, which is the next one, you will understand why it has to be this way.

When my kitten, Bella jumps on the bed, I am so distracted by the pain, I do not see her right away. Then she looks into my eyes to let me know she wants attention. Although I am on different pain medications, after a while they are not as effective as before, so my doctors keep changing them. I am accustomed to the changing of the medicines I have been going through this since the accident. This endless cycle tires me of living, and I want to say, "Lord, please take me now." You may think I would be used to pain by now since I have been experiencing it since the day of the event, but not really. How can anyone get used to pain? It becomes more intense with each passing year; it is like a cloak of misery that I cannot shed. There is no escape! It greets me in the morning and stays during the day and tucks me into bed at night.

Neuropathy comes with burning pain so intense, it feels like someone struck a match and set you on fire. The numbness comes with loss of sensation, which makes it hard to tell if water is too hot, so you have to be very careful not to scald yourself. The tingling is a stinging pain that feels like pins and needles are sticking you.

The nerve damage in my legs causes my feet to burn non-stop! They are sensitive to touch. And there are tingling and numbness, too.

My body temperature is hard to regulate because of nerves damage; it fluctuates from hot to cold. The hotness feels like roasting in an oven, and the coldness is like being in a freezer. These are my spells. When I say to Sweet Baby, "I am having a spell," he knows what is happening. My ceiling fan never stops turning because I sweat profusely.

The neurological disorders have stopped me from traveling because I get sick to my stomach, and my body goes numb and shakes when I ride in an automobile. It is hard to even go 30 minutes from my home to my doctors' appointments. The back seat of our truck is the only place where it is bearable because my mind will not allow me to sit anywhere else.

The mental stress the accident caused me still affects me to this very day. Being in any vehicle gives me a feeling of anxiousness. I will not ride with anyone other than Sweet Baby because he is the only one I trust, and even with him, I can still be wary.

While we are traveling on the dangerous highways, I always pray for God to protect us because I am so afraid of getting into another accident. My body cannot handle anymore traumas, and neither can my mind. I dare not look at the traffic because there are so many bad drivers, and it scares me to see them. My refuge is my home, and if I did not have to go out, I would just stay in. But life does not afford me that luxury; I have to go and see my doctors. Because of my handicaps, which makes me unable to drive, I thank God my husband is my chauffeur. When we return home, a sigh leaves my mouth, and I just want to get settled in. I even talk to my bed by saying, "I am back."

The sorrows of death compassed me, and the pains of hell gat hold upon me: I found trouble and sorrow. (Psalms 116:3 KJV)

I chose this Scripture because I am in a living hell.

5

Depression

My disabilities were worsening, and I was plunged into a state of despondency. Nothing seemed to matter. It was as if I was outside of my body. I screamed, "Let me in!" but to no avail. What is happening here? Who am I? Is this my cross to bear? Then I tried to recall what I had done to deserve this. I prayed to the Lord, "If my pains do not get better, please just let me die." I used to hear people say "a fate worse than death." I did not understand. Now, I do.

Even with the assistance of my husband, it was hard getting out of bed each day, physically and mentally knowing I was facing a life filled with pains. The pains were agonizing and messed with my mind. I just wanted them to go away. I needed a way out. On June 24, 2006, I tried to take my own life by overdosing on my prescription medications. I was rushed to the hospital by the paramedics and had to stay overnight. The next morning, when the doctor came in, he made me promise, I would not try it again.

My niece was by my bedside all night long. She was the one that was involved in the accident with me. I was released in her care because my husband was not available at the time. She brought me home to my husband, so he could take care of me.

I did not keep my promise. On October 8, 2009, I tried it again because three years later after medications and counseling, my pains and mental state were getting worse. I was rushed to the hospital by the paramedics again. But this time it was different. I was not treated as nicely because the staff who cared for me was not as kind-hearted as the one before. I believe they were just there for the money. They did not have compassion whatsoever. During the first attempt, I was handled with warm and tender loving care; the second time, I was treated coldly and spoken to harshly. It literally was a rude awakening for me. At that time, I realized how some people view a person who is bent on self-destruction. Thank God I did not succeed. I will never try that again, no matter what I am going through. Suicide is not the answer.

Some days, sadness comes with a sense of dreadfulness; then I want to retreat into my shell and become withdrawn because I feel hopelessness. Then I get irritated because I do not want these feelings to control me, so I do not let them. I have learned over the years, your thoughts can hold you captive; you can become enthralled in them. The best thing to do is pray and keep your mind focused on God. Please do not think of the worst-case scenario. Do not become depressed because it is a dark and lonely place full of wickedness, which takes on a life of its own.

Loneliness is terrible. I remember being in a crowd of people yet all alone. It is a feeling of forlornness I cannot shake sometimes, but I am grateful it comes and goes. By this, I mean it only visits me and no longer moves in.

When you start to feel down, you have to give yourself a pickup and look for ways to be visible. The main thing is do not let it crush your resolve. When you have to wrestle in your soul, there are other forces that are trying to control you, and they are full of cunning schemes. But do not despair; the light of the Lord can penetrate darkness.

After the accident, I have all kinds of time to let my thoughts be unbridled. Praying and meditating on God's Word have helped me to corral them. I have a tendency to imagine things not as they are. This causes me to be off-kilter in my thinking at times because if I get something straight in my mind, there is no changing it until I see otherwise in my heart. I am saying, I see things with my eyes, but I have an aptitude to not believe them even though I know they are true. But my head has to tell my heart it is okay to relax.

I have a complex mind. Go figure.

A day in the life of mine can be brutal. I call pain my friend because it is with me every day; it radiates from my head down to my feet; it just will not let me go. Burning, numbness, and tingling are with the pains, too. Oh, the agony of it all! My soul is cast down daily! I keep a brave face because my husband has infirmities, too, but he does the best he can to take care of himself, so he can attend to my needs. I am afflicted!

The frigid inside air puts me in a somber mood, and I long for my days of basking in the sunshine. I guess it is like seasonal affective disorder (SAD), a type of depression that different seasons cause.

Bella is a long-haired kitten, and she has to stay cool, so the temperature in my home is set to accommodate her because she overheats easily. A throw covering is kept with me, so I will not get chilled to the bone.

Not a day goes by when I am not in pain. I just found out I need some extensive dental work done because my teeth are shifting. Also, I have temporomandibular joint disorder (TMJ), which makes it difficult to chew because of pain, so I am careful about what I eat. My diet consists mainly of soft foods and soups. Sometimes I do cheat, but I pay for it later.

Talking and dental hygiene is even a problem at times because there are days when I cannot open my mouth at all. I know Sweet Baby likes that! Ha-ha! Just kidding! Also, it causes my ears to ache. Biofeedback can be helpful; it is just another name for mind over matter.

Asking myself, when is it going to stop? Pain overload! But I must be strong because I have come this far by faith. No need for me to cry inside, what good is it going to do? Next; it never ceases. Thank You, Lord, the pains let me know I am yet alive.

O wretched man that I am! who shall deliver me from the body of this death? I thank God through Jesus Christ our Lord. (Romans 7:24-25 KJV)

I figuratively tear at my hair and clothing because of grief and despair, so this Scripture is very befitting to my daily life.

6

Power of Prayer

Faith

I learned the Power of Prayer from my mama because she taught my siblings and me about the Holy Bible. She read it to us before we even knew how to read, and she prayed constantly.

Though I have faith that can move mountains, sometimes I second-guess myself because of insecurities. My heart tells me one thing, and my head tells me otherwise. This is conflicting. The line is easy to be blurred between reality and fantasy. I have learned how to deal with it by the process of elimination and prayer, which gives me faith to make the most of each day no matter how I am feeling. There are days when I do not know if I can make it through, but my faith in God is unwavering and keeps me going.

I can be at my lowest point, but when I cry Abba, Father, my spirit is lifted, and I can feel the presence of Him. I pray to God at all times good and bad, in order that I will be able to receive blessings from above. My spiritual sacrifices to God are through my prayers, and my faith is restored daily.

Daddy and Mama had five boys and five girls; I am the youngest. My second oldest sister nicknamed my youngest brother, Joe (Jody) and me (Buffy) after the kids on the television show…Family Affair. We were always getting into stuff. She has now passed on. Also, she named me (Linda). I have a sister who is my daddy's daughter only, but I love all my siblings the same. One brother and two sisters have passed away, but they are forever in my heart.

There are seven of us left, four brothers and three sisters. My oldest brother is in a nursing home here in our hometown. And my second brother lives with his wife across town. Brother number three lives with his wife on the outskirts of town, and my youngest brother lives close by me. My oldest sister lives in Florence, SC, with her children; second sister lives across town, and my daddy's daughter only lives with her family, in Effingham, SC. None of us strayed too far away from home.

When I was a little girl of two years old, we moved to Winston-Salem, NC. We were there for a year. Next, we moved back to Lake City, SC. After living there for a year, we moved to Olanta, SC, when I was four. Then back to Lake City, SC, at the age of six because it was time for me to start school. Our daddy traveled with the tobacco market each year, and he wanted his family with him.

I was raised in a church my daddy's uncle founded with other members. We had to go to church every Sunday, rain or sunshine. My mama and my second oldest sister sang with the gospel choir, and I sang with the youth choir. My favorite song was "God Told Noah That It's Going to Rain."

When I was young, I had to go to revival meetings Monday through Sunday. We traveled to various churches every week. When I lived with my second oldest sister and her family, she was affiliated with an evangelist, and we followed her everywhere. We went down to the altar, called the mourning bench, every night. The elders prayed and told us to called on Jesus; then we got up and shouted and danced all over the church. My sister and I were 20 years apart in age, so she was like a second mama to me. Growing up, I worked in the cotton, tobacco, and bean fields to have money for clothes, books, and school supplies. Money was scarce, but we got by.

I attended the public schools of Lake City, SC. When I was in elementary school, one of my teachers took me around to the other teachers and students to show them how smart I was. If my mama had let me, I could have advanced to the next grade, but she wanted me to go through all of my grades. In junior high school, I was boy crazy, but I managed to get in some studies as well. When I got to high school, I was very active, ran track, and was a cheerleader. Wanting to try as many things as I could, basketball and baseball both caught my interest. When I tried out for them, I discovered they were not my forte.

As I was growing up, my family and I had many traditions. On Friday, we had fried fish with hot sauce, and rice; on Saturday, we went to the 301 Drive-In Restaurant in Florence, SC. After church on Sunday, we gathered at my second oldest sister's house for dinner; we had fried chicken, rice, collard greens, and dessert. We drank sweet iced tea every day, a favorite of the South. I liked mine with cold milk.

On Christmas, we all met at my mama's house to exchanged gifts and eat dinner.

I walked away from my relationship with God because I was tired of having to go to church all the time. It broke my mama's heart when my fourth oldest sister and I would go to dances at different nightclubs. We partied Thursday through Sunday. My dance card was full because guys always asked me to dance, and I never turned them away.

I graduated from high school, on May 31, 1977. Before graduation, I applied to become a flight attendant. (Back then they were called an airline stewardess.) I was told I was too short, so I gave up on that dream. Then I said to myself, This is not my ending; so I decided to go into the military on the buddy-buddy system. That is where your buddy joins up with you, but my buddy backed out on me the day we were suppose to take the oath.

I was determined to be a good U.S. Army soldier, so I went in on the Delayed Entry Program. That meant I did not have to go in right away. I had so much fun with my friends and family, I decided I was not going in at all. When the time came, for me to report for duty, I did not. Two army personnel came to my home, picked me up and took me to Florence, SC, and put me on a Greyhound bus, so I could report for Basic Training in Columbia, SC.

The night before Induction, the formality by which a civilian is inducted into military service, they gave us cold cuts sandwiches and Mountain Dew soft drinks. Afterward, at bedtime, I boo-hooed all night because of homesickness. The next day, I got fitted for my uniforms, boots, and received all my military gear. I met a cousin and other people from my hometown; then I was okay.

I had one of the nicest Drill Sergeants you can ever hope to have. We were his first platoon of females. I stayed out in the field on bivouac one-night. I had to sleep in a sleeping bag and that was my first time. During the night, I found myself turned away from the opening zipper and I thought I was going to suffocate; I was gulping air and frantic because I could not find the opening; then I started screaming. After that I was detailed to do Kitchen Police (KP). That meant an enlisted man detailed to assist the cooks in a military mess hall. Part of my duty, I was asked to taste the food before it was served. I ate so much and did not gain a pound; life was good. There are many hilarious stories I can tell about my Basic Training. I am chuckling now, just thinking about some of them. My Drill Sergeant even asked me what was I doing in this man's Army. During my time in Basic Training, I met a lot of nice people and some not so nice ones, but that is life in general.

I caught an Amtrak train to Fort Lee, VA, for my Advanced Individual Training (AIT), which consisted of every aspect of storage supply. I had a blast in VA, until it was time for me to move on; then I got robbed of all my money by people who were my closest friends, my roommates. Money I needed to get home on authorized leave and to report to my Permanent Duty Station. That taught me a valuable lesson: Never trust anyone when money is involved. I was so angry, I could have exploded, and I was embarrassed, but I called home and asked for money. My oldest brother, we are 18 years apart in age, so he was like a second daddy to me, gave the money to my mama and she wired it to me. I went home and had a great time with my friends and family. When the time came for me to leave, we were sad, but we know I had to go.

I caught a commercial flight to Fort Hood, TX, for my Permanent Duty Station. But along the way, I had to switch over to a small aircraft; it was very uncomfortable because of close quarters. The roaring of the engine was earsplitting, and I got a bout of airsickness. My Military Occupational Specialty (MOS) was supply. I was assigned to Cold Storage and Dry Storage, where I operated computers on a daily basis. Cold Storage in winter chilled me to the bone; we dressed with many layers of clothing because it was a cold and damp place. Dry Storage in summer was hot and muggy; just being dressed in my uniform, it was still uncomfortable for me. We had these giant fans blowing all the times, but they did not do a lot of good. The heat was smoldering. Outside, you could see it coming off of the pavement.

While I was stationed in Texas, I attended Central Texas College in Copperas Cove, TX, where I majored in Business Administration. I worked in my MOS during the day and went to classes at night. My studies included a course in sociology. Also, I took a course in ceramics, and being a cat lover, the first article I made was of one.

When I was in the military, the best-dressed soldier always got a three-day pass. So I made sure my uniform was always neat, starched, and my boots was spit-and-polish; I always got a three-day pass. My boots were not the Army issued kind; I bought a special pair called jump (paratrooper) boots. In other words, I was a sharp dressed soldier because I took pride in my appearance. That came naturally because my clothes have always been stylish. I was not the materialistic type, but I liked some nice things.

I have always had a bank account, but I really learned how to save when I went into the military. There was so much money in my account, it made my head spin. In the Army, there is a type of retail store called the Post Exchange (PX), and everything in it, at that time, was so cheap. Four years earlier, my fourth oldest sister had fraternal twins. My niece, Stephanie, who was involved with me in the accident, was one of them. I bought all kinds of clothes from the PX for my sister's twins and shipped them home to Mama because she and Daddy raised them.

My money and I were soon parted because I was a fool. My friends in the service told their sob stories to me, and I loaned them money and never got it back. I became freehanded in the military because growing up, I was so stingy and selfish. I decided to make a change.

My room door was always locked. I played with my paper dolls, baby dolls, and coloring books by myself. When I went to the store and got back home, I ate my goodies and did not offer them to anyone. So, I became a softie and got taken for my money by my friends.

What I learned from all those experiences is, I have a giving heart. And now, when I see people in need, I reach out to them. Some offer to pay me back and do. Others do not. Whichever way, I will not let it change me because I love the person I came to be. I'd rather give than receive. Some people might take my kindness for weakness, but I do not see it that way.

My enlistment was completed on February 16, 1981. During my enlistment, I received letters of appreciation, and various medals of honor. I was selected to go to Officer Candidate School (OCS). The military offered me an opportunity to go to Hawaii for six months to see if I really wanted to get out of the Army. I wanted to go to Hawaii, but my mama got sick, and my sister called and said mama needed me to come home. I received an Honorable Discharge, and that was the end of my military career.

The entire time, when I was in the military, my mama did not once greet me or see me off at the train station, airport or bus station. She was desperately afraid of airplanes and could not bear to see me leave. But when I came home to stay, I took a bus. When the bus door opened, there she was waiting to welcome me. Mama was overjoyed because I was home to stay at long last. It is true; there is no love greater than the way she felt for me.

I returned home to Lake City, SC, and started working as a computer operator for various companies. Also, I attended Francis Marion College in Florence, SC, where I took courses in early childhood development and creative writing. But I majored in Computer Science.

My mama died at age 69 on May 2, 1990. There are times when it seems afresh, and I find myself sitting by her bedside seeing her take the last breath. I do not know if it was due to me grieving or if it was real. I was crying, shaking her, and saying, "Wake up, Mama"; then for a moment, I saw her chest rise again. Silence, then it dropped; she was gone. I cannot explain it any better than this. It was the saddest day of my life. My mama was the most beautiful, sweetest, meekest, and kindest soul I have ever known. The matriarch of our family, and the mother of the church I grew up in. What a gentle and quiet spirit she had. She had so many friends but knew how to mind her own business.

I never heard her said any bad words or saw her do any wrong. I was told by her, if you cannot speak good about a person, keep your mouth shut. Also, she said to me it was not good for a girl to show her teeth all the time; it might attract the wrong person. Because she was always loving, caring, and generous, she never met a stranger. Everyone who came in contact with her loved her. I miss her every day. Thank You, God, for blessing me with a mama of that caliber.

My daddy died at age 95, on August 16, 2016. I miss him every day. He was my friend whom I could always depend on for anything. Many times, I would have fallen flat on my face and given up without him. I would cough up any amount of money just to see his handsome face and hear his laughter again. He stood taller than most with a slender built. I liked the way he used to crossed his legs and clasp his hands together; that made him look distinguished to me.

He was the father of the church I grew up in. We attended church service and when we sat next to each other; he gave me money to put in the offering plate because I was always broke. I was an adult with responsibilities and never had any extra cash. He put gas in my car, and we would ride all over creation. When I visited him at his home, he told me very true but funny stories about people he knew. He was a great storyteller with a wonderful sense of humor. If I could only have those days back. Thank You, God, for giving me so many happy years with him.

I came back to my faith in God after my car accident. I started reading the Holy Bible again. Though I have had great experiences in my life, the greatest has been reading the Holy Bible from Genesis to Revelation. I was told if I had gotten to the intersection a minute sooner, the car would have collapsed on me because the car I was driving was two-seated had a safety bar, which prevented the top from caving in, and because of that, my life was spared. God was watching out for me even when I was not serving Him like I should.

One reason why I could not open the driver's door was because the car was a total loss. The nerves are so badly damaged in my hands was the other reason. This may sound strange, but it was the best day of my life because it gave me a chance to come back full circle to Jesus Christ. I am now God fearing. Every day I am trying to live a life that is pleasing in His sight and make Heaven my home. My ears are always tuned-in to a good and inspiring sermon on my church's conference line. I treat people like how I need and want to be treated. Of course, I know this alone will not get me into Heaven, but right now, it is food for my soul. I used to find myself reminiscing about the good old days, but these are better days because I am in Christ. The journey I am on now, I pray to see it to the end. I am not expecting to receive a pot of gold, but a crown of pure gold.

Prayer and faith can turn the impossible into the possible. I was taught this many years ago from my religious upbringing. There were days when I had no idea how my situation was going to turn out, so I began to pray and believe through faith, and the answer came from an unexpected source. What I am saying is, praying with faith can change things.

Your Heavenly Father loves you and is always there to see you through anything you have to face.

I always tell myself, there is not anything I have to face that God and I cannot handle.

Now faith is the substance of things hoped for, the evidence of things not seen. (Hebrews 11:1 KJV)

This Scripture encourages me to keep praying for my reward.

Strength

After the accident, the times when I tried to commit suicide, I was suffering from debilitating pains in my mind and body. I could not see a reason to be in this world because each day I was waking up to nothingness. Did I even exist? Someone else should have been taking the air I breathed. What is my purpose? With each dawn of a new day, I still struggle with finding the answer. Because sometimes I wonder, when is my change going to come? Life can be so difficult to bear at times, but God's protective bubble is a hedge around me.

I have learned fear will stop you from trying. It can paralyze you, but you must work even harder to conquer it. You have to wholeheartedly tell yourself to never give up, and mean it.

I know about the benefits of praying when pains, fears, worries, heartaches, disappointments, and so forth, come. They are a part of life; you have to fortify yourself and deal with them. Some of them can rattle you to no end, but you have to regain your composure and keep going in spite of your obstacles. Because with living comes many unforeseen issues, be girded and look for answers. Do not become defeated before trying. There is strength in the face of adversity because it makes you learn how to live with your problems and look for ways to figure them out. The answer is not clear-cut in every circumstances. Some situations are more involved than others. In those times, you may have to reach deep inside to find a solution. I have learned no matter how big a problem is, there is some kind of resolution. You just need to be levelheaded and deal with the issue at hand. Though it is hard, find the strength to go forth and take back your life. A long time ago, my mama prepared me for the battle. She said to me "You are a soldier." Her words gave me the courage to keep fighting, even when the odds are stacked against me.

As far as I am concerned, I will keep battling until I have no fight left in me. I am a soldier trying to win a war, even though I am facing a formidable opponent—pain—who does not have any intention of calling a cease-fire. This battle has been going on for a very long time now. And with each passing year, it gets tougher. Even though I have on my full armor, I grow testy at times. So, I pull out the big gun, the Holy Bible. I summon my prayer warriors, my friends and family. Defeat is not an option, for I will never surrender. I am renewed in my spirit and uplifted by God; He gives me the strength to keep on living.

I can do all things through Christ which strengtheneth me. (Philippians 4:13 KJV)

I can carry on because of Him; that is what I derive from this Scripture.

Endurance

The accident left me not being able to cope with my problems. Each day was getting harder, I was struggling to live with myself. What is the use? I just wanted to give in. Having to wake up each morning and go through the day and into the night with chronic nerve pain and other medical conditions, you develop a protective layer like an armadillo shell because that is the only way to survive. I always say, the Lord and I know better than anyone else what I encounter in my living. Of course, Sweet Baby knows a great deal about it, but not all.

I had to find the inner strength to endure my trials and tribulations, so I started to read the Holy Bible and was encouraged to read it daily.

With each passing day, I grew stronger, so I kept on reading; then I found the endurance I needed. In His Word, I am rooted and grounded. This gives me the strength of mind to carry on regardless. And I seek after the things of Him, so my life can be a witness for Him. Thank You, Dear God, You are always there when I need You most.

Beareth all things, believeth all things, hopeth all things, endureth all things. (1 Corinthians 13:7 KJV)

I have endured so much, and I am still struggling, but love is strengthening me. That is why this Scripture resonates with me.

Patience

Being disabled all these years from the accident, I had to disciplined myself to not be anxious for anything. Patience came from never-ending days and bloodshot eyes from sleepless nights. I did not know one day from the next; they all seemed to run together. There was a time when I used to become sick from worrying about when things were going to happen. Lying in bed made me believe things that were not real. My mind was not at rest, so I lost my grasp on reality.

I was a proofreader at one time, so my job consisted of me being patient with a sharp perception of things, but after the accident, it all slipped away. Then the Holy Bible taught me about true patience, long-suffering (something I can attest to), because I am still going through my struggle.

I have learned how to pace myself and realize things transpire in their own time. But it is still hard for me to concentrate sometimes because I wanted things done yesterday. Complaining comes easy because I can be so impatient and expect things to be done right away. Sadly, most things in life do not pan out that way. I have to wait for the outcome, and this causes me to be restless sometimes.

While I am waiting for my change in life to come, I have learned perseverance. I know that is what it takes to withstand some of the hard times. It is not easy to be still when I want to see desired results right now. It is hard not to start screaming out loud. Inside, it is like a volcano about to erupt! I try to fill each day by thinking positive and expecting the best by God's grace.

> But let patience have her perfect work, that ye may be perfect and entire, wanting nothing. (James 1:4 KJV)

I am waiting for my road to come to an end, this Scripture translates there is something better for me.

Hope

Hope, I have always had, but the accident tested it. Along the way, I lost hope because my medical conditions were not improving. It took me many years to realize things will get better, no matter how bad they seemed. Every day, I thank God for my husband, the love of my life, my Sweet Baby, because he will not let me quit. He encourages me to fight harder, and he is always there at my beck and call. Sometimes I wonder if dying is better than living. When that thought crosses my mind, I know it is an attack of the enemy.

I have learned to overcome the lies of the enemy. When he tells me there is no way out and to just lose hope, I press in harder to what I know to be true: God is able to strengthen me for what is ahead. I am a living witness to let others know that if they keep pressing forward, put God first and foremost, everything else will fall into place.

I thank the Lord for another day; for Him allowing me to open my eyes; and for all His blessings He has already bestowed upon Sweet Baby and me. We know that He has more to shower on us. This gives me hope to trust and believe in His Word and His promise, that I will never be alone or forgotten. Even though there are times when I still want to give up, I will continue to keep fighting. It is a hellacious battle, but I am trying to be victorious.

I see the beauty, hear the sounds, and smell the fragrance of God's creation. The lovely flowers blooming, birds singing, the lonesome wail of a loon, and the smell of fresh-cut roses, etc., make me thrilled about life and give me hope.

My *hope* for the rest of my life is to keep the *patience* God blessed me with during the *endurance* I gained from my troubles through the *strength* by His inner working power and the *faith* which I reaped those many years ago from a true woman of God, my mama

And for God to please keep breath in my husband's body and never stop the blessings and watch over him forever.

And for God to bless my friends and family always, and everyone else in the world.

I pray in Jesus' name,

Amen.

> For to him that is joined to all the living there is hope: for
> a living dog is better than a dead lion. (Ecclesiastes 9:4 KJV)

As long as I have breath I have a chance, this Scripture makes me want to keep trying.

7

Food Preparation

From the moment I learned Sweet Baby was a Certified Chef, he has been preparing all of our meals. When we first met, some of the foods he cooked, I had never tasted before. Like shark steak—to my surprise, it was delicious. He introduced my palate to fine cuisine. I was not that great of a cook from the start, but I did know enough to not starve.

Sweet Baby says I am not good in the kitchen, and this makes me happy. Because I am unable to cook, he prepares delicious meals for us. One of my favorites is lemon pepper baked rock Cornish hen, rice seasoned with the hen's drippings, and chopped collard greens seasoned with applewood smoked bacon. Another favorite is teriyaki baked salmon, homemade mashed potatoes with sour cream and chive, and buttered sweet corn. He also cooks healthy foods. Most of the time, he changes his menu just to satisfy me. Sometimes, I holler inside, Why can I not help him? It is unfair for him to be put in that position. Then I remember: My husband loves to cook, so be grateful.

On my birthday in 2021, he cooked a succulent roasted red pepper glazed duck, buttered rice seasoned with the duck's drippings, steamed cabbage seasoned with hog jowls, and homemade potato salad. I feasted on it for two days. My mouth is watering for more; I can hardly wait until he cooks another meal like that one! I love his cooking and the appetizing way he presents his food. My husband treats me like royalty because he said, I am his Queen. He can cook anything my heart desires. And he bakes cakes and pies, too.

There are mainly four types of meat: Poultry, beef, pork, and fish. Sweet Baby knows how to prepare each one of them to perfection.

As much as I love his cooking, over the years, my dietary needs have changed significantly. Due to my irritable bowel syndrome (IBS), he is always concerned about what is best for me. We eat a lot of baked, sautéed, and grilled foods. There was a time when I was able to eat anything I desired. Now everything has to be prepared to not irritate my sensitive stomach. This is becoming old to me. It also makes me sad because I wish I could eat anything again.

My husband cooks the most beautiful and best tasting eggs I have ever eaten. I did not know eggs could be so yellow, fluffy, and delicious. In the South, we have a tradition most people do not like. We eat chitterlings, known as hog intestines, and a lot of people find this to be gross. That is not a problem for me; I just know they are a delicacy. Sweet Baby fixes them in a way, so there is no stinky smell in the house. They are ready to be eaten in 45 minutes because he is the fastest chef around.

His grilled top sirloin steak is so juicy and tender, it will melt in your mouth. I was raised up eating fried chicken gizzards, but Sweet Baby stewed some because of my dental problems. My first time eating them that way definitely will not be my last time. I love them! They were so soft and moist, I had a second helping.

My husband was taught at the Johnson &Wales Culinary Arts School. When he was in the U.S. Navy, he was the Head Chef aboard a submarine. After all those years, he still has not lost his touch.

Sweet Baby is an amazing person, whom I admire. He has done so much in his years of living. He was also an engineer with CSX railroad. I love to listen to him tell of his experiences. He has traveled so many places abroad. My husband can do all kinds of things. By far, he is the most intriguing person I know. God blessed me with a wonderful husband, and I am thankful for him every day.

Dietary Challenges

My major dietary changes came about when I met Sherryl Johnson-Hanna, Registered Dietitian, on Facebook. Under "People You May Know," her profile kept coming up. When I connected with her, she informed me about smaller portion sizes, gluten-free diet, non-dairy milk, ground flaxseed, and probiotics. The difference she has made in my life cannot be described.

God can send the right person to us when we need them.

Smaller Portions

I was already eating small portions because everything I ate and drank caused excruciating pains and burning sensations in my belly due to my severe stomach ailments from having irritable bowel syndrome (IBS). When you have this condition, portion sizes are a must, and the types of foods you eat can make it better or worse. My immobility makes my IBS worse because that is when it became a serious bowel issue. I have had digestive problems for so long, I cannot remember when they started. But if I make a guess, I would say back in 2004, when my gastroenterologist diagnosed me with colitis.

I had to learned how to eat smaller portions to lessen my conditions. Eating in this manner also keeps my weight even-keeled. Recently, I am having more inflammation in my belly than normal. It is very painful and causing me a lot of distress. My diet was already cut back to smaller portions. But now, I have to eat even less than usual. I have to manage my weight, and because of my IBS, TMJ, and recent dental problems, I am losing weight, and that is not good for me. My menu is getting shorter, so it is becoming very frustrating to me. Also, it is harder for my husband to prepare our meals. Sometimes, I feel like I am wasting away to nothing. But I know that, too, is an attack of the enemy.

Gluten-Free
The only kind of bread I eat is gluten-free. Since making this change, I have noticed that I am less bloated and less gassy. I eat it with a plant-based butter.

I try to avoid any grains with wheat, rye, and barley, because gluten is found primarily in those types of grains.

What Is A Gluten-Free Diet?

Gluten is a specific type of protein that you will not find in meat or eggs.

You Have Gluten-Free Bread Choices

An assortment of breads, and gluten-free products are found in many health foods stores, and all major supermarkets. These are often made with rice or potato flour. Please check the label to be sure it says 100% gluten-free.

Medically Reviewed by Kathleen M. Zelman, MPH, RD, LD on December 17, 2020. http://www.webmd.com/

Non-Dairy

The only kind of milk I drink is non-dairy because some of them are low in added sugars; saturated fats; and provide calcium, protein, and vitamin D. I drink a plant-based milk, which is nutritious, delicious, a good source of protein, and lower in sugar. It has as much protein as cow's milk.

There are many different non-dairy products to choose from. Just go to the dairy section of your local supermarket, and pick out whichever one(s) is/are best for you. If you do not see them, ask, because sometimes they are kept in a separate section of the market.

Ground Flaxseed

Ground flaxseed is a great source of fiber. I eat it on everything and drink it in hot coffee. It is tasteless, low in calories, and has protein, omega-3, and omega-6 fats. Also, it is supposed to be good for hot flashes and night sweats. And I find it helps with constipation.

The Dirty Deets

Flax seeds need to be ground up in order to release their nutrients, because they are coated in shells that serve as armor against your digestive system.

By Keri Glassman, MS, RD, CDN
http://www.webmd.com/

Probiotics

I take a daily probiotic for my digestive health, which is a microorganism I consume in a dietary supplement. It maintains or restores beneficial bacteria to my digestive tract. Yogurt is also a good source to maintain a healthy balance in your belly.

What Are Probiotics?

Probiotics are especially good for your digestive system, because they are live bacteria and yeasts. Researchers are trying to figure out exactly how they work. Please ask your doctor about which might best help you, because all have different benefits.

Medically Reviewed by Sabrina Felson, MD on July 30, 2020
http://www.webmd.com/

I was diagnosed by my gastroenterologist some years ago with irritable bowel syndrome (IBS), a painful and maddening condition. I was prescribed all kinds of laxatives, but none of them worked until I was prescribed a daily laxative and other medications. I am still seeing my doctor because it is a never-ending cycle. The pains and burning sensations in my belly are unbearable; then there are the bloating, cramping, and gas. Not to mention constipation and diarrhea.

I try not to be stressed because it adds to the problems, so when my head begins to throb, my heart starts to ache, and my hands become wet, I pray even harder. Dwelling on everything that is going on in my body can become weariness, and that leads to depression; the gateway to the darkness. I do not want to go back into evilness untold. It is like being dragged down into a black hole. You are fighting with all your might not to go into a very bad and scary place. The only thing all of these things do is make my life miserable.

I had a doctor's appointment with my gastroenterologist on June 22, 2021. My blood pressure first reading was 89/57, and the second one was 97/62. It was low. What now? Also, I have to prep, drink two bottles of solution, for a CT scan scheduled for seven days later. My doctor wanted to find out what was going on inside of my abdomen and pelvis. But I am not complaining; I am just thanking God for life.

My Sweet Baby is always here for me. I cannot make it without him. Words do not come close to the feeling I have in my heart for him. It is like my heart swells and overflows with love.

The results of my CT scan showed a lot of inflammation in my gut. I conferred with my registered dietitian, and she informed me to try more bland foods, such as fish and white meat opposed to red meat. Also, sugar can increase inflammation, and as a general rule, plant-based foods are anti-inflammatory, and animal foods are more inflammatory. Basically, it is trial and error.

My CT scan also revealed that I needed a procedure done. The procedure was performed by the surgeon, on August 4, 2021, and I was informed there is no cure for my stomach ailments. A biopsy was also done by the same surgeon. I am just so blessed to have my devoted companion, Sweet Baby, and my loyal kitten, Bella. And much to my delight, my great-nephew, Stephfon, who is like a son to my husband and me, has been spending sometime with me.

Sweet Baby and I almost raised him from a baby. Also, my great-niece, Stephfora, has graced me with her presence, too. I named her (Stephfora). They are the children of my niece, Stephanie; she was involved with me in the accident.

It is August 27, 2021. With each passing day, my health is deteriorating, and there is not an answer to the question. I cannot even ask why.

In life, you never know what is going to happen to you.

If you had told me I would end up this way, I would have laughed in your face and called you crazy. But the joke is on me.

Here I am, broken-down and busted. Undone by difficult situations and unpleasant experiences because of the accident.

This is how I feel most of the time, but I am holding on by God's grace.

I said earlier, I did not let anyone or anything worry me that was out of my control. A devil-may-care attitude, having a relaxed or casual manner.

Correction: I do not let anyone or anything worry me at all because God is in control and in charge of my life. At times, I feel there is no rest for the weary. Me.

Even though I have Sweet Baby and the support of others, there is something inside of me that keeps nudging and jostling me at the same time to hang in there. So, I do.

During my second suicide attempt, the fear of dying took over me, and I called 911 myself for help. But now, any day the Lord calls me, I am ready for my departure because my spiritual bags are packed, and my house is in order. The fear of death is gone.

The Holy Bible tells me to eat, drink, and be merry because tomorrow I may die. I believe what it says.

Now I am about to get raw with you.

There is something seriously wrong going on inside of my body. I have not had a bowel movement in eight days. A little man is in my stomach, tying it up in knots. He is ferocious! It is very painful to eat and drink, and merriment is nowhere to be found.

My registered dietitian told me about a balanced nutritional drink; it is mainly keeping me alive. Although the pain and burning are intense, I eat some soup and soft foods, but very little. And I am in touch with my doctor.

But I believe if this keeps going on, I will surely die.

I trust God, no matter what.

It is August 29, 2021. Ten days since I have had a bowel movement, but something deep inside of me will not let me worry about what is happening inside of me. To be candid, I am tired. Sometimes when I wake up, I am sad knowing I have to face another day of pains and depression and everything else that comes along with these two conditions, and the other medical conditions that are plaguing me.

For I feel like all my work on this earth is done.

God has been good to me.

I have had a good life for the most part.

A long time ago, I learned how to take my hard knocks. Because I said, you roll with the punches or lay down and die. I chose to roll with the punches. But I am tired of rolling now.

Do not get me wrong; I know suicide is not the answer. I am saying, when my number is called, I am ready to answer. On the other hand, I am praying for a brighter future because I am not ready to leave Sweet Baby, Bella, and some friends and family behind. So, sometimes when God opens my eyes and I see I am still here, I get happy and ready to face the day whether being good, bad, or indifferent. I know this is a mixture of opposing feelings, but I cannot help the way I view living now.

Well, my friends, I had my follow-up appointment on September 1, 2021, with my gastroenterologist, after my procedure was done. My blood pressure was 85/54.

I have pan-ulcerative colitis, inflammatory bowel disease (IBD). It started in my rectum and spread to my colon. My entire colon is red, inflamed, and swollen. The pains and burning are excruciating in my gut and rectum. And I have all my other medical conditions to contend with also. With this new disease, I have started a journey to a new and unknown land, a place called the point of no return.

Once again, my quality of life has changed.

At least I now know what is causing me more misery in my gut than normal. The pain is vicious, and the burning is like a flame that cannot be snuffed out. And much of the time, I am nauseated. It is hard to concentrate on anything but the persistent suffering I am undergoing. Also, it is difficult for me not to become disillusioned with life. Because one thing after another is happening with me, but I choose to press forward, regardless of the bumps and bruises along the way. Asking myself, when is it going to end? But through it all, by God's grace, I am okay. Because I have life, and as long as I do, there is hope. Thank You, Lord, for the covering over me that only You can provide.

The thief cometh not, but for to steal, and to kill, and to destroy. (John 10:10 KJV)

To have faith, strength, and not give up, that is what this Scripture means to me.

8

Emotional Support

Sweet Baby has always been my leaning post. After the accident, I would sometimes get overwhelmed. I stayed in bed and pulled the covers over me for days. I could not seem to get myself back to where I was before because I only saw the negative side of things. He motivated me by using his military voice. I knew he meant business because he served in four branches of the U.S. Armed Forces.

Sweet Baby served in the Air Force as a Pilot, and in the Army as an Airborne Ranger. Also, in the Navy as a Head Chef, and in the Marine Corps as a Military Policeman. When he enlisted, the government allowed him to serve in different branches. He completed his enlistment in each branch. And received an Honorable Discharge from each one.

With his stern voice, he would say, "Act like a Christian instead of professing to be one. Do not let the devil steal your spirit; there is no truth in him, because he is a liar." Satan wanted me to keep doubting and pitying myself. The love and emotional support from my husband keeps me going. I am in love with him, and after all these years, I am still thrilled to be his wife! He is the first person I want to see when God opens my eyes at the beginning of a new day, and the last when He closes them at the ending of the day. True love is beautiful! My husband is a precious gem, a rare treasure that is hard to find, and I am so glad we found each other.

We have our moments, just like any old married persons, but we have experienced more happiness than sadness. Through it all, he is still the one. My biggest fear is living after Sweet Baby has passed away. I do not know if it is a sin for me to hope I die first, but I hate to think about what would become of me without him. No one else is going to treat me better, I know that much. I cannot put into words, what a difference, he has made in my life since the first day we met. It took me 39 years to find him. When I was young, I had often wondered who would be on the porch with me, watching our lives go by. I am so glad it is him. God blessed me with a loving, caring, faithful, and wonderful companion to share life together.

In elementary school, I read a lot of fairy tales, about how the prince and princess lived happily ever after, and knights in shining armor riding in on white horses. All of them had happy endings, but none of those can compare to the happiness I am experiencing now. This poem says exactly how I feel:

"I was made and meant to look for you and wait for you and become yours forever." – Robert Browning (1812-1889)

A few days ago, we had a health scare. My husband's blood sugar went up very high. The number was not even a reading on the monitor. Praise God, it is back to normal now. When we realized to the extent it was, I was devastated because if anything bad was to happen to him,

I would be like a ship on a stormy sea…just listing. This means that my life would be lopsided. And he is the wind that keep my sails afloat.

I would be amiss, not to mention the support from my friends and family. The circle of them all brings love and joy into my heart. They always push me to never give up. The reason I need and want to keep going is because of them. Some of their lives without me would be so much harder because I check on them to see if they need anything. It is deep-rooted in my mind and heart to do good.

My inspiration comes from God, Who gives me the revelation to make an impact on people's lives, especially my loved ones. When I am able to help, it gives me comfort like being cuddled in a cozy blanket. Also, it causes my heart to leap with gladness. Putting others before myself is what my mama taught me, and I know it is the godly thing to do. The wellbeing of my friends and family is very important to me. Seeing smiles on their faces and knowing their spirits have been uplifted warms my heart. I used to worry about them so much until my heart was restless. Then I found a way by working on myself through God to just pray and leave them in His hands.

My closest friends and family call me after each doctor's appointment, just to see how I am doing. It makes me happy, and on my worst days, I am okay knowing they care. What a blessing it is for them to take a few minutes of their time for me. My niece, Stephanie, I nicknamed her hunny bunny, and I communicate daily; she is one of my most loyal supporters, next to Sweet Baby. I could not love her any better if she was my very own. She has been with me through so much and still is right here. My other most loyal supporter is my stepdaughter, Ashley, I nicknamed her daughter. When we first met, we liked each other and became friends right away. Also, I could not love her any better if she was my very own. Her husband, Albert, I nicknamed him son, is a Captain in the U.S. Air Force. Because they move often, I do not get to see them as much. But I thank God we can stay in touch by phone from miles away. The love I feel in my heart for all of them cannot be put into words. I pray to God, asking Him to keep them all in my life for many more years to come.

Even though I have the support of my friends and family, the Holy Spirit that dwells within me, is greater than anything I have to face.

Ye are of God, little children, and have overcome them: because greater is he that is in you, than he that is in the world. (1 John 4:4 KJV)

God's Holy Spirit has equipped me for any obstacles that are placed in my way; that is what this Scripture imparts to me.

9

Love Beyond Measure

Primary Caregiver
　　When I realized I could not take care of myself after the accident, I was overcome by guilt; it was like a millstone around my neck. I stopped eating and became anorexic because I was so distressed. Everything had to be done to suit me because I was always fussy about details. No one could do it better, so I thought, until it could not be done by me. My life turned into an annoyance, for Sweet Baby and me.

　　I was always an independent person, which made me a bit selfish, so I had to learned how to become subdued and submissive. Sometimes, you can be too independent for your own good, so I found out. When the time came and I needed help, I wanted to refuse it. I was only fooling myself. I had to buckle in and accept that I could not make it by myself. The days of independence were over for me.

　　My husband stepped up and rallied around me because I lost my self-esteem and confidence. I dared not to make a move without him. I could not even think for myself. My mind was jumbled, and everything seemed incapable of being surmounted. Sometimes, I escape from reality by watching classic black-and-white movies, but this was not one of them; this was my real life. He has always been there for me, but now, he is the number one player in the production of my life. I had no idea our life would come to the point where I depend on him so greatly for everything.

I first met Roy Crosby on May 18, 1998, when I called the Lake City police to have someone removed from my home. He was one of the officers who responded. When I saw him, said to myself, Wow! I did not know Lake City had an officer that looked so good. It was love at first sight. I know superficial charms can be shallowness, but I just could not help myself. He looked as if he was of mixed heritage, light complexion, naturally curly hair, and a nicely groomed face.

His uniform was heavily starched with clean, black patent leather shoes. I liked what I saw, and to top it off, he performed his duty professionally. The guy he was there to remove told Roy he would leave. Officer Crosby said, "I know you are leaving because you are riding with me." Then Officer Crosby gave me his card and told me if I needed to come to the station, have the dispatcher call him on the radio. I gave it some thought. After a few hours had passed, I went to the station to asked him to please get a phone card and give it to the guy, so he could call his job.

I knew in my heart Roy was going to be my next boyfriend. I looked at him while he was talking and said to myself, Why can I not have a guy like him? His lusty lips looked kissable; they tempted me, and his manly cologne awakened my senses. Then I thought he is married, so I gave the money to him for the phone card and left.

The next morning, around 6:00 AM, my doorbell rang. I answered the door. It was raining. There stood Officer Crosby in his raincoat and black patent leather shoes, glistening in the moonlight. He asked me if I was okay;

then I invited him in. We stood in the kitchen and talked, and it seemed like we knew each other forever. He asked me, did I like fish? I said yes. Four days later, he brought two fish sandwiches by, and we sat at the table, talked, drank soft drinks, and ate. He gave me a hug, and it sure felt good to have his arms around me. At that moment, I knew we were kindred spirits. I had to have him! He asked for his card that he gave me earlier, wrote his home number on it, then left. I called him seven days later, on Memorial Day, and his mama answered the phone. He was living with her after being transferred from another police station to Lake City. I asked to speak with him. According to his mama, he was not available. Click. She hung up on me. When I went back to work after the holiday, I called his job. The dispatcher told me he was on the night shift, and she would give him my message. We began a loving relationship from then on.

We got engaged on Christmas Day, 1998. I was speechless, and when the words came, I said, "It is about time. What took you so long?" My heart had a home, and I started crying because the guessing about my future was over, and my best friend wanted to marry me.

The ring was 14K yellow gold, baguette shaped, with multi rows of diamonds.

Shortly after our engagement, Sweet Baby took some time off from policing and started driving over-the-road trucks transporting hazardous materials. We traveled all over the U.S. and Canada. There was a bridge in Ohio, Little Miami River Bridge; it literally took our breath away, because it was 239 feet tall and suspended from a long hydraulic arm. We drove across the Louisiana bayou, which was 375 miles long, stretching across Arkansas and Louisiana and boasting more than 100 different types of fishes.

An original deep-dish pizza, we ate in Chicago, and in Philadelphia, we ate an original cheesesteak sandwich. We have been to places where most people have only dreamt about, and we have souvenirs to show of our travels. On the Royal Caribbean Cruise Line, we went to Nassau, Bahamas. Once there, we took a seaplane to view the island; it was picturesque, but I got a bout of airsickness. The underwater excursion was like something I had never witnessed before. Seeing the different marine animals was an amazing adventure.

Our taste buds were stimulated by the taste of different exotic foods and drinks. We went downtown Nassau and street shopped buying t-shirts galore. The memories still bring me joy today, thinking of our time on the sea together.

When we became a couple, Sweet Baby took charge over all of our finances. I did not have a budget, so he stepped in and put things in order. We started pooling our resources. After the accident, we had a change in status, for the worse temporarily, but by God's grace we persevered. I am grateful to God that Sweet Baby was able to maintain all of our expenses on a policeman's salary.

Financial stress can be a common factor after a horrific accident. Many are left unable to work, and their finances are ruined. Living within your means definitely become a necessity. When the medical bills start to accumulate, even with insurance the deductible, out-of-pocket expenses can be substantial. It is in your best interest to have money to tide you over. If there is not a lot of savings, this can be difficult. Many things have to be rearranged to fit your budget because the income and savings you once had will dwindled. The hospital bill consists of things you may have never heard of, and you will get charged for everything down to a box of tissues. All of that could put added pressure on a relationship and cause some conflicts, but if the relationship is stable, a resolution can be found. Along the way, there will be disagreements, disappointments, and setbacks; you just need the mind-set and tenacity to stand as a united front.

Sweet Baby and I made a commitment to each other. We will do life together. Whether in the valley, climbing the hill, or on top of the mountain, we promised each other we would do it as one. Because of the accident and everything that came from it, we wondered many days what was to become of us dollars-and-cents wise. It was not easy, but Sweet Baby made it all work.

After an accident, it might take years to recover financially because medical bills and prescription drugs can be costly. Even some over-the-counter medicines can cost a lot. If this happens, arrange an installment plan to meet your obligations. It will take longer to pay your debts, but you can keep on eating because you will have money for food and other household expenses. You might have to set up a few payment plans, so you can budget everything. If it comes to this, just cut back on some things to get by. Please know that if you are consistent, the penny-pinching period will come to an end.

Roy's Point of View

Before the accident my girlfriend, Linda, Sweet Baby (we call each other the same nickname), was always active and energetic. We had a good life; I am not saying our life is bad now, but we were not disabled.

We would get dressed up and attend weddings. On one occasion, we left one of my best friends' weddings and went grocery shopping. The people in the store thought we were ballroom dancers; we were flattered, but we told the truth.

Linda would wear her heels and had the most gorgeous legs. She was a sight to behold. Her inner and outer beauty radiated like the sun. She will always be my Queen.

Do I believe life as we knew it is over? Will she ever walk again? What are we going to do now? Is this how it is going to be for the rest of our lives? There must be something that can be done. But what? The questions never stop invading my thoughts.

Linda is becoming very difficult, and I do not know how much longer, I can take this; nothing seems to please her. Dear God, please give me the strength to carry on because she needs me. This is my daily prayer to my Heavenly Father.

Okay, we have to adjusted to our new life; we can get through this by God's grace. When we took our vows, I said in sickness and in health, for better or for worse, so no matter what it takes, I will honor my vow; I am here to stay. She may be difficult at times, but I love her; we are joined at the hips. After all these years, I cannot imagine life without her.

…End of Roy's Point of View

We got married three years, and three days later, on his birthday. We have been inseparable ever since. When we first took our vows, it was the Justice of the Peace and us. Thirteen years later, we renewed our vows in our church before 75 guests, some of our closest friends and family. Sweet Baby plays six strings bass guitars in our church. During the ceremony, he played "When I Said I Do," by Kenny Lattimore & Chanté Moore while he was sitting and looking into my eyes. I was touched beyond words. It was a full moonlit evening when we arrived at our reception supper (I always call my evening meal supper). Our wedding colors were black and ivory with a splash of red; the venue was decorated with the same colors. The guests were dressed in the colors also. It was a magical evening, and it seemed like something out of a fairy tale. I will treasure the memory for the rest of my life.

After our vow renewal, Sweet Baby and I moved forward with every day living. There are valleys and mountains along the way, but we trust

God for better things. We are looking ahead for what He has for us. With Him at the helm, there will be smooth sailing with the rough waters that we have to navigate. I prayed for many years for God to send me some-one who could love, respect, accept me for my faults and misgivings.

Eccentricity has always been a part of me, but it has worsened since the accident. By this, I mean my mind travels to places I dare not tread. This can be frightening at times! My heart starts pounding like crazy, I cannot think, and I forget where I am. It feels like a parallel universe. I thank God I am better able to control my thoughts now because at first, they scared me to no end. I have learned how to distinguished what is real from what is not true. My saving grace is prayer.

It is not too revealing for me to share my feelings, considering all I have to contend with to get through this thing called life. Some days, it seems as if I just want to say, "Lord, give me rest at the close of the day, for I want my work in this world to be done." But then I think about how would my husband and loved ones would feel being without me. So, I pray and ask the Lord for peace and strength for my continuous battle.

My pains are unyielding, for they do not let up. But I must stay in the fray because, in the end, I hope to win. It does not take much to quit; I attempted suicide twice, but never will again. In spite of all I am going through, life is beautiful.

With Sweet Baby as my primary caregiver, I know he has my best interests at heart. I trust him undoubtedly. He always tries to do what makes me happy because his love for me is unconditional. Mutual love, respect, and trust are the keys to our happy marriage and lasting affec-tion for each other. He gives me the courage to withstand anything I have to face. Knowing he is there to rescue me, a warm and safe feeling overtakes me, because it is not easy for me, since my life has been changed so drastically for the worse.

I know, oftentimes, taking care of me is tiring for my husband. But he is steadfast and diligent. Not to mention, I am hard to please on some occasions. But over the years, I have learned humbleness and graciousness. I feel anyone else would have given me over to a nursing home or facility of that sort a long time ago. When we found out my medical conditions were regressing, he told me he was going to take care of me in our home. Since then, his health has declined also. But he is still devoted to me and my care.

When I need something, Sweet Baby does not hesitate to get it, be it food, clothing, or shoes. He has given me so much; we have run out of space to store it all. Mind you, I am not ungrateful; he is a great provider. I do not lack for anything; he always considers me before himself. He really takes good care of me. Imagining life without him is not something I want to think about. Just the thought sends shivers through me. My t-shirt says it best:

BLESSED by God,
SPOILED by my husband.

We are in the process of buying another house or renovating our current home because we have outgrown our humble abode. We have known this for a while now. But sometimes, you can want things so badly, and it is not what God has intended for you yet. So, we are waiting patiently for the blessing until He sees fit to give it to us. I never forget to be thankful. We are blessed abundantly according to His Word.

Some days, I am filled with guilt for not being able to be the wife Sweet Baby needs me to be. It weighs on me so heavily until, sometimes, it feels like my heart is going to burst wide open. And being in bed more often than not, it seems like there is nowhere to run from the anguish. I have to say to myself, What happened to me is through no fault of my own. Knowing this eases my conscience, somewhat, but not fully. Because he is sick also but still has to do the entire running of our home by himself.

Hear my cry, O God; attend unto my prayer. From the end of the earth will I cry unto thee, when my heart is overwhelmed: lead me to the rock that is higher than I. (Psalms 61:1-2 KJV)

This is my go-to Scripture when guilt is overtaking my very being.

10

Sweet Baby

I have never had a relationship with anyone like I do with Sweet Baby. When it comes down to it, he is my everything. He is a good and decent person. There is no one else I'd rather spend my time with than him.

I used to always feel insecure in high-end places and around highfalutin people because I felt I was not good or pretty enough. It took me many years to love myself. Sweet Baby showed me the person I could become if I put forth the effort by changing the way I think of myself with a new and improved mindset. A good enough and decent human being. His words permeated my senses; they made me know I was capable of being mended. I had to be unplugged and recharged. Sometimes, your mind has to be jolted to understand the real meaning of things.

People complimented me, but I thought it was just flattery.

I had no problem getting a boyfriend; they always approached me first. There are two things I can get, I used to say to my friends and family, a job and a guy, and it had been like that from day one. Guys have always been attracted to me. At first, this was a mystery to me.

I became boy crazy at 13 years of age and did not stop being that way until I met Roy H. Crosby, my true love.

My mama used to tell me it was not good to jump from pillar to post in a hurried and disorganized way; that led to things that could have been avoided. At the time, I was too pigheaded to realize what she was telling me.

Being with Sweet Baby is as if I never was with anyone else before. It is the best feeling in the world for me to wake up and see his sweet face.

I thank God for him every day.

Also, I love waking up and seeing baby Bella because right above our head, my kitten lies. My bed has a space behind the headboard that stretches from end-to-end, and when God opens my eyes after sparing me to see another morning, that is where she can be found; she loves high places.

There was a time when I was obsessed about what people thought of me, and how they saw me when they laid eyes on me. Sweet Baby changed all of that for me; he made me feel beautiful and gave me confidence. I felt as if I could have conquered the world.

Years ago, I read a book titled Get Rid of Him because I was going through some changes in another relationship—not the one mentioned in the "Love Beyond Measure" chapter. This was a 12-year relationship that was full of more downs than ups.

To make my point, there was a chapter in the book saying how to tell if a man was a good one and if he was marriage material. Everything the book told me to look for, I found in Roy. In other words, Sweet Baby checked all the boxes.

He treated me like his Queen from the start, for I had never felt a love so deeply.

Yes, I had other loves, so I thought. But that is another story; not for this time.

Right now, I am speaking of Sweet Baby, my one and only.

When we first became acquainted, I heard negative things spoken about him, then I realized that was because he was a no-nonsense type of police officer and did not let many people into his world. So, I decided to get to know him for myself. It was the second best decision I had ever made. The only one better was accepting Jesus Christ as my personal Savior.

Sweet Baby and I are each other's best friend; I like the way we communicate because we can talk about anything, even our past relationships with others, and there is no jealousy or hurt feelings when we do.

Because of the accident, I had to stop being a whole wife to him intimately a long time ago. But that is okay between us, for we are just happy to be together in any capacity; both of us are permanently and totally disabled now.

Maintaining our home, and vehicles, and everything that comes with them, are our top priority, so we do not dwell on anything else. And baby Bella always keeps us occupied. In a nutshell, we have learned how to be content with the curveball that was thrown to us. We have a solid foundation; God has truly blessed our love.

He is not a romantic guy, so he rarely says he loves me, but that is okay. Because his actions speak volumes. I say I love you to him all the time. But we are individuals with our own preferences. I could not be happy with a clone of me.

To sum it all up, we listen to and understand each other. Also, we are honest, open, and patient with each other. And we put the other before ourselves. But I have more patience than him. Most of all, we are in love.

I kissed some frogs to get to my prince; they were just mere stepping-stones.

What God has for you; it is yours!

Nevertheless let every one of you in particular so love his wife even as himself; and the wife see that she reverence her husband. (Ephesians 5:33 KJV)

My husband, I adore, that is why I love this Scripture.

11

Inspiration

My Sunshine

As I stated earlier, I am a cat lover. Belle came into my life as my Christmas present in 2006. I was at a very low point. It was six months after I tried to kill myself. Sweet Baby got her to brighten my miserable existence. What a ray of sunshine! She gave me a reason to live again. Each day, excitement welled up in me when she jumped up on my bed and I saw her sweet face. Laying on my chest and gently scratching my eyelids was how she woke me up. I had envisioned drawing her because she was beautiful with many different colors. Also, she was so happy and full of love and laughter. I watched her grew from a three-month-old kitten into a full-grown cat.

She was my faithful companion and could sense when my day was hectic. When I had a doctor's appointment and we returned, she would be sitting at the door to welcome us back home. She loved unconditionally. When my baby got sick, all her get-up-and-go went, but she still had a gleam in her multi-colored eyes. It was heart-wrenching to see her clinging so hard to life. I prayed for God to take her away from the pain, and I asked some of my closest friends and family to do the same. She is no more. My beloved Belle, (also known as Princess Belle), an indoor cat, Maine Coon of 14-plus years passed away on January 5, 2021.

We are still grief-stricken. It is hard to believe she is gone. Sweet Baby and I tried to make the most of each day. Our life was filled with anguish untold. I cried every day no matter how I wanted the well to run dry. I phoned my Pastor regularly and asked for prayers. That old nasty stinking cancer took her away from us, and she is buried in our backyard.

I did not want another pet after the passing of my beloved Belle, but Sweet Baby kept saying he needed a kitten. At first, I did not agree with him about getting another one because I said my heart could not go through hurt like that again. He wore me down, but I had two stipulations: it had to be a female and not calico colored. He wanted a male and did not care what color, as long as it was a full-blooded Maine Coon. After much discussion, we made plans to get another furbaby. It took some doing, and we were skeptical at first because of so many internet scams.

The reason I did not want a male is because they mark their territory by pissing on things. After we came to an agreement, we went online and began searching. Then I saw Nikol, now known as baby Bella. My heart skipped a beat; I had to have her pronto! We were uncertain because earlier we got scammed out of a large amount of money from a crook in New Jersey. Nikol was coming from Russia. The breeder in Maine convinced us she was legitimate, and so was the breeder in Russia.

Finally, we got our next ray of sunshine. Our indoor kitten arrived on March 12, 2021. Her name is baby Bella. She is a full-blooded Maine

Coon, black and tan with a tinge of red, and hazel eyes that change colors. Her fur is silky and smooth. She purrs with her soft voice. Although she is only five-months-old, she looks like a full-grown cat. Her breed got its name because it is specifically native to the state of Maine and has a brush-like tail that resembles the tail of the raccoon. Maine Coons grow to be strong and huge. It is the official state cat of Maine. I read that they naturally produce a fishy, musky smell, but mine smells like a lilac in springtime.

She was flown from Russia, so she has a Russian passport. Then to Maine, where she had a week's stay in Maine where she got all of her shots. From there to North Carolina, and then to us in South Carolina. My baby did some serious traveling to make it into our loving and waiting arms. She is so sweet, playful, and has breathed new life into our home. She has carved a place in our hearts that, at first, I was unwilling to open.

I find having a pet is very therapeutic for me because if I am having a bad day, she still loves me unconditionally. When I look at my baby, my heart overflows with joy, and the cares of the day melt away. I love her more than words can say.

Please, do not forget a pet—I prefer cats—can be very therapeutic.

My beloved Belle brought out the best in me. She was the calm in my storms and the illumination in my darkness. I could always count on her to put a smile on my gloomy face. She is gone, but forever on my mind and always in my heart.

Now here comes baby Bella, a delightful addition to our family. She is hilarious. Bella likes to show her prowess by running, jumping, and kicking her toys around like a soccer ball. There is never a dull moment in our home these days. She is a climber and likes to sit high. Our new baby is helping us to gradually adjust to the fact our beloved Belle is gone; we thank God for many wonderful years with her.

We must move on to the next chapter with baby Bella, who is gorgeous, nosy, and always getting into stuff. She really makes my day and chases my blues away. Baby Bella keeps me laughing. What a blessing she is to me after the passing of my beloved Belle. She is about to eat us out of a house and a home, but we treasure her. We pray, God bless her with good health, long life, and many happy years with us.

I love my furbabies.

Bella is my pride and joy. Getting her was the best thing Sweet Baby and I could have done. She not only cheers me up, but him as well. I hate to say this, but she is the sweetest and gentlest kitten we ever had.

Our first furbaby Belle was sweet and gentle, but very temperamental. At times, she was standoffish, but we chalked it up to her getting older. We have yet to see if Bella is going to turn out the same way. She is a little over nine months, and weighs 16.3 pounds. On average, female Maine Coons weigh between 8 to 12 pounds, but they can get much heavier. Bella is already over that weight. She eats like a pig. But Sweet Baby and I do not mind. We just want her to be healthy and happy. We say, let her eat. She is giving us so much happiness. Her ability to be quick and agile is like something I have never seen. I know that I mentioned this before, but she really is the sweetest pet we have ever owned.

Lord, I pray she stays the way she is now for many years to come.

Many studies have shown that having a cat can calm nerves, lower blood pressure, help prevent and treat cardiovascular disease, cancer and chronic pain, strengthen the immune system and even help you live longer. (https://www.catsnap.org>display)

Another thing that is therapeutic is the scent of lavender. The smell is soothing and can change my mood. Many years ago, I found out about its calming effects and its sleep-inducing properties. There are so many different products, such as soaps, lotions, candles, and crystals, just to name a few; I have them all. Visualize this: A hot bubble bath surrounded by burning candles, in a dimly lit atmosphere; you are so at peace within because the heat has melted your cares. You can see them going down the drain one by one, and everything feels wonderful. That is what the scent of lavender does for me.

Lavender essential oil is one of the most popular and versatile essential oils used in aromatherapy. Distilled from the plant Lavandula angustifolia, the oil promotes relaxation and believed to treat anxiety, fungal infections, allergies, depression, insomnia, eczema, nausea, and menstrual cramps. (https://www.verywellmind.com)

Intellectual people also inspire me, as they impart wisdom to me. My husband is the first person I turn to for this because he is so fascinating. His knowledge of the world is astonishing. I have learned so many things from him that I never knew. When he speaks of those things I am not aware of, I am like a little kid hanging on every word. When he told me the reason water rolls off of a duck's back is because the ducks feathers are oily, and oil and water do not mix, it fascinated me. Then he told me birds eat the seeds off of the weeds to survive, and the lightning always comes before the thunder. He loves to share nuggets of wisdom with me as much as I enjoy listening. He has taught me so many things that no one else taught me before. A long time ago, a man told me love is a misunderstanding between two fools. Well, a fool, I must be—because I am in love with my husband.

Also, a good church sermon inspires me; I am so blessed to know the Holy Bible because I can relate to the preaching. I listen to Bible messages daily. Some of my favorite preachers are Dr. Charles Stanley and Dr. David Jeremiah.

It is always good to know the Word of God for yourself, so no one can lead you astray.

What works for me, may or may not, work for you.

A righteous man regardeth the life of his beast. (Proverbs 12:10 KJV)

I loved my cat, Belle, and I love my kitten, Bella, so this Scripture is near and dear to my heart.

12

Peace

My peace comes from the Word of God because it speaks of His goodness, mercy, and forgiveness for a sinner like me. I am a Christian, but as a human, I do make mistakes. Though I pray constantly, I stumble, too, because it is easy to do, living in this world of sin and sorrow.

There was a point in my life where peace did not abide, no matter how I longed for it. My very being was tormented, and I could not see an end in sight. I searched for light and found darkness—and oh, how great it was! I prayed for mercy, and forgiveness, and the Lord pitied me.

Life changes, but the Word of the Lord is forever. I am so enraptured to know I have a place where I can always find comfort and encouraging words.

When I think about how good the Lord is to me, my soul cries out hallelujah. One of my favorite t-shirts says exactly how I feel:

It Is Well With My Soul.

It resonates that sentiment. I had to get out of my own way and let God have His way in my life. At first, it was hard to do because I was so used to doing things in a manner that suited me. But no matter what I did, all came to naught. When I submitted to Him, l found peace. I truly believe the Bible when it tells me that there is nothing too hard for God. No problems are so big He cannot solve. My prayer every day is to ask Him to let His will be done in my life.

Seek peace through God, and you will find shelter from the storm. There are so many bad things happening in today's society. When the storms of life come—and they will—we need to be anchored to weather them. Some of them are worse than others, but we have to be prepared for all of them. When the strong wind starts to blow, what better sturdy shelter than our Lord and Savior Jesus Christ?

When my storms of life are raging, I run to my safe haven: God. I have not found a better place. He hides and protects me, and I am confident that He will continue to do so.

The various sounds of nature, such as the steady pitter-patter of the raindrops falling on the roof, the waves crashing against the shore, etc., lull me to sleep. I like to awake to the birds chirping in the trees and the lonesome mournful cry of the loon. These things give me comfort and peace also.

Sometimes, I feel I am unmerited of God's blessings. It is miraculous to me how He turns bad situations into good ones. Over the years, I have gotten myself into circumstances where I could not see a way out of, but God altered them. He has done this so many times for me. And He keeps blessing me still.

Peace of Mind

There is nothing like having peace of mind. It had bypassed me for a very long period. Every day was full of uncertainties; it was like being in a snake pit waiting for the next strike. I was having anxiety and panic attacks, one right after the other. I just wanted to let go of life. All I saw was dark clouds rolling in.

Where is the sunshine? How much more can I stand? Help! I am drowning, please save me! Then salvation came. Each day, my burdens became less; I was able to smile again. Once I started immersing myself in the Word of God, my mindset changed. My mama used to talk about peace that flows like a river. I found it after I allowed God to be the head of my life; what a happy time in my life, and I have been swimming in peace ever since. Whatever comes, so be it. I am indifferent to a lot of things now because I cannot afford to have my peace taken away. It is my lifeline; I am holding on. When it feels like I am losing my grip, His Word is a place of refuge.

Reading the Holy Bible calms the inner workings that still try to tear at my soul. It gives me a serene feeling and comforts my mind. I would be lost without God's Holy Word. Believing in it has taken me to inexplicable heights.

The understanding is too vast for me to say, for I am in awe. His power is helping me through my struggles. By shutting some things out, I have learned how to slow things down in my life. Having mindless time for myself is a necessity for me. I thank God I have learned how to train my brain to take a break.

Many thoughts and voices sometimes hit me unmercifully at one time. If I listened to them all, I would be a nervous wreck. I am most grateful to be under my doctors' care by being helped with medications. But I never forget to pray. Living can be so complicated sometimes, but I find contentment in being a believer of His. My peace of mind comes from knowing I am never alone. God is awesome! He is better to me than I am to myself. When I need a place of solace, His Word is the answer.

I start with turning the television off, not answering the phone, and blocking out all other interferences. Then I go into what I call my sweet hour of prayer.

During this time, I meditate and satiate on Holy Scriptures. I have learned when I get anxious or afraid to go in the Holy Bible to allay these emotions. Not only for these two feelings, but for all of them. God's mercy is endless.

I strive to live godly every day. It is not easy, for there are so many stumbling blocks trying to deter me. I am blessed to have Sweet Baby in my life; he keeps me on the right path and makes sure the way is clear for me. I will love him to the last breath!

I'd rather have peace of mind than any amount of money in the world. Some people may beg to differ because they think monetary gain brings happiness. Do not get me wrong; I know it takes dollars-and-cents for living, but I am speaking from a personal experience. For I have been to hell and back. Doing time in my own purgatory, money did not do me any good. If that was the case, I never would have become depressed and tried to commit suicide twice. The devil had me under his feet and tried to destroy me. But God said, "Not so, take your hand off of my child!" That is why I am here today to tell my story.

I thank God for sparing me from myself. During those times, I was my own worst enemy; I was listening to the voice of the devil. Thank God I now know His voice from the enemy's.

The older I get, the less I tolerate conflict, drama, and any intense situations. I want peace and as much happiness as a person like me can have for the rest of my life. When I think back, there are a lot of things I would have done differently.

But as we know hindsight means just what it says. There is no going back for a redo. We have to advance, or we are marking time.

It seems like I am going nowhere fast sometimes. But as long as I am above ground and not taking a dirt nap, that is okay. I will continue to pray and meditate on God's Word because I find peace within when I do.

My spirit soars up to Heaven, and when it comes back down, I am weightless and revitalized to face another day. Yes, I get weary many times, but I push it aside and keep going because, at the end of the day, that is the best thing for me. Dwelling on it would eat at me like a cancer.

The Lord gives me peace when my mind is troubled because He gives me strength day and night. I would be lost without Him. I am nothing; no one. Some days, I lose consciousness of time and place. It takes me some time to get things straight in my head, and my heart has to catch up. Then my world is righted again.

I am at peace knowing I have a roof to keep me out of the rain, food to nourish my body, and clothes to hide my nakedness. There is so much destituteness around the globe, and I know things could be worst for me. When I see how good God is to me, tears of joy cloud my eyes, and my heart fills with gratitude.

Conversing on the phone with certain people gives me peace. Hearing inspiring and uplifting words spoken to me, and speaking them in return, makes my heart smile. But straightforwardness is the best way for me; I do not talk to anyone with honey dripping from my tongue. And I expect the same from them, for that can do more harm than good. I do not intentionally hurt anyone's feelings, but when I speak the truth, I find inner peace.

My favorite day is Sunday, for it is the time when I am most at peace. After my sweet hour of prayer, I shut down my mind to everyone except my husband, Roy, and my kitten, Bella. We are in a world of our own. I am thankful for the quietness and peacefulness because they invigorate me for my everyday existence. Without these times, my life would be in a shambles.

Also, I find peace being a country girl because I am down-to-earth, mild-mannered, not high-maintenance, and not materialistic. I prefer country living because I find it more peaceful than city life. For I have been to many places, but none can compare to my home state. There is no other place I'd rather be than the state of South Carolina, where I was born and bred, and that is where I want to die.

And take the helmet of salvation, and the sword of the Spirit, which is the word of God. (Ephesians 6:17 KJV)

I find peace when I read the Scriptures.

Epilogue

What I learned about the power of prayer, and being disabled with a good support system, is that there are days when life seems unfair. Why do I have to go through all these changes? I have to take a regimen of medications and supplements just to get through the days and nights. Restful sleep eludes me more than not. I have to always be conscious of my diet. Then I say to myself, Why not? You are alive. God gave you another chance; He sheltered and shielded you when you were living outside of Jesus Christ, the Ark of Safety. Be grateful, because there are so many people worse off than you. Thank God for breath. Now is the time to tell your story; be committed to helping others by sharing parts of your life. After a conversation suggesting that I should tell my story, it was placed upon my heart to let others know they, too, can live a meaningful life after a life changing event.

My life is meaningful and blessed because I keep God as the focal point of my existence. I thank Him every day for Sweet Baby, my family, my doctors, my registered dietitian, and my friends. Without them, I would not have the support I desperately need. Through them, I am motivated to be more present when facing adversity instead of shying away. They are loving, kind-hearted, and caring people who want the best for me. I can always count on them; they are just good, down-to-earth folks. Miracles come in all colors, shapes, forms, and sizes; I believe the good and kind people God placed in my life are my miracles.

None of us can live in this world alone; we need each other for many different reasons. It is wonderful to have people you can depend on when you need a helping hand and just to hear words of kindness. You need people who will stay during the storms; not just when the sun is shining. Always surround yourself with positive relationships because negativity can place a damper on your life. Associate yourself with people who use words to build you up and not tear you down because you are already having a rough time. You need someone who is going to administer to an ailing person.

Use the Word of God to guide you through your tempest; you will not find a better shelter, and there will be comforts you need that can be applied to your living. Any accident victim who is going through a difficult time need as many resources as you can stand.

Follow through in all you do, and please do not be misdirected by anyone.

When my medical conditions first started to regress, my husband persuaded me to give it all I had, so I did. He purchased every exercise machine you can think of, but I was unable to use them because of relentless pain. Years came and left, but still no progress; so my health and spirit began to wane.

If you are reading this, you know some of the in-betweens. Many years later, I am still battling, but that is okay, too, because it means I still have breath. Each time I am blessed to wake up, I have to brazenly fight an uphill battle; one day, I am looking to win the war.

My book is being written during the coronavirus pandemic. Sweet Baby and I have been fully vaccinated. I try to keep my mind focused on happy and positive things, but we know sad and negative doings happen also. With all the other unrests already in the world, the virus brings so much death and destruction. It is very depressing to hear about how many lives have been lost and families shattered. My family was visited by it, too. My heart goes out to everyone who has been affected, and you are in my prayers.

When the cares of life cause you to feel helpless, the best thing to do is pray. And if you can lend a hand, please do so because there are so many people in need. You cannot fix the world's dark problems, but you can lighten someone's eyes by showing them they are not alone.

You may not have been in a car accident, per se, but are needing a breakthrough from some other crisis you are facing. I am a living witness saying you can withstand anything by God's grace, mercy, truth, and loving-kindness. You have to pray, and believe, and diligently meditate on His Word, because faith can move mountains. And please always remember, God blessed the doctors with the knowledge to heal the sick. Also, you will need prayer warriors, so do not be ashamed of asking your friends and family to lift you up in their prayers.

I know prayer changes things for the betterment. So, in my conclusion, I put God first and foremost; I do not forget to pray, and I am blessed beyond measure, to have a loving and caring spouse. I take the good advice of my healthcare professionals; I also depend on my friends and family.

I am showing how it is to live as a permanently and totally disabled person through the power of prayer and a good support system.

You can too.

On June 24, 2006, I tried to take my own life. It was just another day faced with pains and uncertainties. I woke up feeling lost and confused. So I said, "Enough! I cannot take anymore of this melancholia! Living is meaningless!" When the time came for me to take my morning medicines, I took a handful of pills and washed them down with water. Then I laid out and waited for death. I was awakened by the ringing of the doorbell. A friend of mine called my husband, and he called some of his police buddies, and they called the paramedics. The battle in my mind is still raging, but I must carry on. If you read the "Depression" chapter, you know the ending of the story.

Grieving about your heydays are futile, and it can only lead to heartaches. Gather the pieces of what you have left and do your very best to advance into the next chapter of life. You might find it is not too bad once you and your caregiver(s) come up with routines to make life easier for you and them. I am not saying it will not be an obstacle course because I would be lying. All I can tell you is never give in! Keep fighting! Because it is a battle.

Remember, God is in the miracle making business. He is still opening blind eyes, making the lame walk and the dumb talk. For He gave the doctors the power to accomplish these things. If you are going through a crisis, the very first name to call on is the name of Jesus Christ.

My Lord and Master in Heaven is God, and I know He loves me. I have put my hand in the Master's hand, and asked Him to lead the way.

God gives us a chance to begin anew each day; in His eyes each morning is the beginning. What a blessing it is for me to be among the living! I try to live with dignity, honor, and by doing the things that are pleasing in His sight. Because I am God fearing.

I try to place the best impression possible stamp on my life, so that people can see me as a good, kind-hearted, and decent human being. And a significant part of their lives. I do not waste a moment on what might have been because there is no expiration code on dreams, and time waits for no one; the clock never stops ticking.

You need to evolve with the moment at hand.

I have learned how to be relaxed, refreshed, restored, and renewed in my spirit by the Word of God, and prayer. And I always dream for a day of jubilation when I can break out of my prison of pain.

My friends, try to not dwell on the past. We can learn from our mistakes; I know I have. My past has helped shape my present, and now, I know what not to do in the future. The key is not to linger in the past long, and when you do visit, do it for the right reason, which will be a lesson learned. But do not wallow in grief and regret. Live in the moment, concentrating on the present. It may be difficult, but do the best you can and keep your eyes forward.

As I was writing this book, numinous things happened that left me shocked. I cannot explain them; they could not have been just sheer coincidences. They had to be God's doings.

Writing my book has given me a new look inside of myself. I thought I knew who I was, but I had no idea of the breadth, depth, and height of being me.

I am damaged and ruptured beyond repair, but I am still here. I am like a bird perching on the edge of euphoric and an unhappy destiny, but through God, I will triumph.

Through faith and prayer, and with the help of Sweet Baby and Bella, I am mustering the strength to look ahead and not behind. Though each day the road seems to get longer and more unforgiving, I am still hopeful.

I wanted to share my story in this book hoping it will bless, encourage, and make a difference in those who read it, and help them as they navigate life's changing challenges.

I am now an empty vessel!

Peace I leave with you, my peace I give unto you: not as the world giveth, give I unto you. Let not your heart be troubled, neither let it be afraid. (John 14:27 KJV)

God wants you to have peace, and my sincere prayer, and desire are for you to have peace also, so this Scripture sums that up.

God Bless,
An Accident Survivor

Resources and References

National Suicide Prevention Lifeline:

Hours: Available 24 hours.

Languages: English, Spanish.

Toll free: 800-273-8255

Dietary:

If you do not have a Registered Dietitian, you can contact your local hospital or doctor's office for help.

Chronic Pain:

The American Chronic Pain Association. Website: https://www.theacpa.org

WebMD. Website: http://www.webmd.com/

*A free, one-time registration is required in order to view the full linked article and all other content on the Medscape/WebMD sites.

Therapy Cats – Catsnap. Website: https://www.catsnap.org>display

Verywell Mind. "The Health Benefits of Lavender Essential Oil." https://www.verywellmind.com

Also, you can find helpful information by searching the internet.

Disclaimer:

Please check with your physician before adding or changing anything concerning your physician's treatment plan.